By Artrelle Raydine Merriwether Hunter

Acknowledgements

*First giving Honor to my **Lord and Savior Jesus the Christ** who is my true everything. Had it not been for The Father, that gave His only begotten Son and through His love, His compassion, His grace and mercy, His peace, His joy, His strength, His salvation, His hope, His glory, His sacrifice, His blood, and knowing you for who you are; this day would not be possible. It is your Holy Spirit living in me and your Word in the scriptures that gives me life, ability, knowledge and wisdom that I can share and express my true hurt as you my God witnessed on Calvary. Through my living testimony as first a Christ seeker that others reconcile their lives back to the same cross that gives us life and gives it more abundantly than we can ever think or ask. So, I thank you matchless King-for being my bread of life that through it ALL, you are truly my ALL and ALL!!!*

This book is dedicated To: My loving dear daughter: *Lamenah Merriwether*, my cornerstone and kind son: *Lonnie Moses Merriwether*, my beautiful mother: *Julia Mae Merriwether* and my concerned caring brother: *Darryl Van Curtis Merriwether*. My beautiful granddaughters, *Laurelle (Ellie) Grace* and *LaShelle (Shellie) Faith Garcia,* affectionately known as my 'Tinkys'. Although none of you knew of my intent to write this book, I dedicate it to you for always supporting me, uplifting me and believing in me through all the hurt. You listened and heard my cries, saw the tears and you genuinely felt sorry and expressed that "God will…" My pain was sometimes on the weight of your shoulders when Mama departed. I thank you for praying for me and adding to the peace that I needed. I love you all to life and I thank God for us being a part of each other. Our family circle will always be surrounded in and with the love of God.

A Personal Thank You

I thank God all the time-But I must publicly thank the person who made him known to me:

I honestly must say openly that I truly THANK the illustrious and esteemed *Bishop Joseph Nathaniel Williams Sr.*; Founder and Pastor of the Christ Church International of Jamaica, Queens, New York. I received my deliverance and became saved under your prophetic and prolific teachings and I am sorry that I left so prematurely in 2005. I never left or lost the fact that you made Jesus and the scriptures plain to me and that led me to a new life with Christ. I personally, professionally, privately and publicly Love Him. I never left the Word! So, Thank you awesome Man of God. I see you as a man of valor, distinction, Integrity, faith and most importantly, servant leader. It is by His grace and His mercy you introduced Him to me back in 1997 and I joined a great ministry under your leadership in 1998. You offered Romans 12:1-2. I pray your understanding and forgiveness that I was misled and did not stay. BUT PRAISE BE TO GOD I DID NOT STRAY FROM THE HOLY SPIRIT!!!

Ephesians 1:11-12 - In him we have obtained an inheritance, having been predestined according to the purpose of him who works all things according to the counsel of his will, 12 so that we who were the first to hope in Christ might be to the praise of his glory.

Just a few more scriptures that describe the character, your mindset, your attributes and a vessel and true and faithful servant. Blessed be the name of our God and God bless you Bishop!

Ephesians 4:11 - *And he gave some, apostles; and some, prophets; and some, evangelists; and some, pastors and teachers;*

Isaiah 55:4 - *Behold, I have given him [for] a witness to the people, a leader and commander to the people.*

1 Timothy 5:17 - *Let the elders that rule well be counted worthy of double honour, especially they who labour in the word and doctrine.*

Thank You

To **Rev. Jose Torres,** President of United Chaplains, State of New York for having a vision of Chaplaincy and to expand God's kingdom. You truly embody the teachings and the importance of being a chaplain for the people of God.

To **Rev. William T. Armstead,** Pastor of First Church of God in Christ, Queens, NY for operating as the clergy liaison for NYPD. Thank you for encouraging me to take a more active involvement in the 113th and also introducing my husband and I to the civilian police academy.

To the entire *113th Precinct* for being a bridge of officers in every capacity and in every unit-I can't list each name independently but you all know who you are. You are not just about the uniform or blue but about community change, diversity and putting the people first. Your first line is to help. That is so greatly appreciated. If I may say especially to my dearest **Det. Tanya Duhaney** (Community affairs advocate) you are the pillar of what it means "to go above and beyond."

To my "sistah" **Tracie Michelle,** you are my family, my friend and confidant. I extend to you my most vigorous thanks for first encouraging me for so long to write and put my story out there. You have inspired me so much and I truly thank you ever so much. As an author of so many books, I appreciate that push and how you inspired me with Godly wisdom, pure family friendship and most of all love.

To my dearest **Dorothy N. McCain,** accomplished author and entrepreneur, I thank you because as your book came out, I was already in the process of writing. Speaking with you further inspired me and you shared how I should pursue and complete my story as well. That was touching and moving.

To my "brotha" **Minister Neal Wright,** first for being a true and longtime old friend from when we were kids. You have believed in me for oh so long and you have told me time and time again, write your book, preach God's word, and always study His Word/Bible. You have taught me kingdom values and shared your capacity of ministry and from the bottom of my heart I appreciate your kind and caring spirit and most of all your brotherly love for me and the God we serve. I can hear you 'my sister just do it'.

To my friend for life **Rev. Patricia Williams,** I can't even begin to express the gratitude I have for our friendship and journey together. We've been friends from knee high and you've allowed me becoming your child's godmother. But the gift that God has placed on your life is exemplary. What can I say, you knew this even before I saw it coming? Bless you my love and thank you most of all for always being there always listening always understanding and always saying, "continue on Gods path."

To my bestie, **Susan Ann Bobian** of 50 years since knee high toddlers. We've been through a lot, the fire, the storms and survived it ALL. Thank you for believing, entrusting, and buying me my first pair of red bottom shoes and told me 'I want you to preach in these!' I did that October; there are so many things I can thank you for; so let me thank you now for everything. You have been a true and righteous friend. Who can ask for a better one? One Love Sue Bee! I simply love you to life and know I love you endlessly.

Family Value

Family is forever, I thank God for all of you; and being a part of *Merriwether, McCain, Foster, and Hunter!* Love you ALL....

I just simply need to thank my loving aunt who offered me Jesus in 1996, and told me that nobody and no-one would or could ever change me other than Jesus. You said "so come on and go to church with me" and I did. Shortly after, I attended my first women's conference with you and there is where I experienced a real breakthrough. *Gaynelle Merriwether* you were absolutely right! And I will never forget it! Thank you and may God continue to spare you!

I sincerely thank each one of you with all my heart and with all my love and with all of Christ... *Thank you! Thank you!! Thank you!!!*

A Humble Thank You

To "The Church" congregants/members. Thank you always for your love, gracious and kind support down through the years. How you would turn out in numbers when I preach. You would show up at any event to always support me with words of encouragement. To my dearest Spiritual mother – you know who you are - a Jesus gem, thank you lovely and godly lady. I can go on with a list of so many of you and you know it. I believe each of you know who you are, and how much I truly love you ALL. To those who I have had the pleasure serving with on the Compassionate Ministry Team, thank you for sharing the same compassionate God!

Expressions

To the nurturing *Pastor Sean Cort and* his company**, True Perspective Publishing House. I** truly cannot thank you enough for your insight and your professional expertise. Your concepts and the context you brought into making this project happen was outstanding. This would not have been possible without your effortless passion, assistance and awesome work in bringing this to pass. I just thank God for the late esteemed Bishop Williams for this connection and wonderful introduction.

A Special Thank You

Richard S. Hunter: To my God fearing, kind loving husband of 14 plus years and the best man known to God that one woman could love for the past 20 years. Thank you for choosing me as your wife. I don't take this lightly and I don't take it for granted and all our family and friends know all too well. I have myself a winner in you. When God made you, He really broke the mold. I couldn't thank God for a better husband, partner, lover, and friend.

I don't mean to sound like it's all that – when the truth is, it is just "ALL THAT" Everyone knows it! You're rare, a different yet special kind of life partner. I couldn't and wouldn't change that for the world. You have blessed my life from the moment we began officially dating in May of 1999. A distinct, smart, analytical man with integrity, loyalty and some of the best qualifications God can give a man. How I appreciate how dedicated you are to me. I am so trusting of you. Our years of marriage is filled with so much fun, laughter and pure happiness. I just adore you and the company you have given me the last 20 God given years. No matter where we go what we do, you are my heartbeat, my lifeline, the ideal species in the form of a man on God's creation. I love you truly and unconditionally.

May God continue to soar in you, man of valor, my husband, my ride or die, the other half and best part of me.

The God in you is faithful to believe. I pray you never change. I have a good thing and that good thing is you! I love you to life for the rest of my life.

I could not imagine my life without you. God blesses! All the best!!!

But I want you to understand that the head of every man is Christ, the head of a wife is her husband, and the head of Christ is God. 1 Corinthians 11:3

Loving Christ! Loving Life!!!

CHURCH HURT – SPOKEN WORD

Some don't know what it's like.

Having troubling thoughts that keep you up all night.

To morn for your wife

While she still has life.

Physically above ground and alive

Yet lost her spiritual drive.

The blessed breath needed to keep her living,

A consequence of adversaries who are driven.

By Satan and his ungodly ways

Surrounded by people who are afraid to say,

Or call it for what it is.

Because they too are followers of his.

Church Hurt caused by those who have lost religious focus,

Allowed by those who fail to see what is obvious, false, and bogus.

It should never be this difficult

To serve in any house that God built.

Yet here we are

Dressing the wounds inflicted by those who are supposed to protect us

Partly due to their inability to respect us.

The other part would be the disappointment

Of knowing this isn't what God meant.

How dare they disrespect God's word

With empty actions,

Judging and awarding God's servants based on their satisfactions.

This makes the entire system flawed

And oh my Lord

What other choices do we have left?

So we stay longer

When we should have left,

Allowing that Hurt Seed to take root

Resulting in an unholy hemorrhage

Causing all sorts of internal damage.

As a husband I put pressure on the wound in an effort to stop the bleeding,

However, what do I do if I can't provide enough spiritual feeding,

Enough nourishment to revive her and bring her back?

From the Church Hurt and Spiritual Attack,

Church was so much easier before I got involved.

A thankless experience if the wrong people are allowed

To revolve, circling around like vultures examining their prey.

As they pray on you instead of for you.

All while pretending to adore you,

Hoping to turn you into a living corpse.

Church Hurt has marriages concluding in divorce.

Honorable men must measure their response

To preserve their congregational reputation.

Can't always reveal the total truth in your proclamation,

I estimate the casualties before I address the inflammatory.

You can't know the full hurt when it occurs

Because the lines get blurred.

Often one gets numb to it

So, your true purpose you forget.

Pain and anguish now become your language and resistance, your existence.

Your Christian walk becomes a limp.

Fearful each step may cause you to trip,

On eggshells is your new walk,

One of now that you no longer talk.

Church Hurt will deny you the courage to speak up and stand strong

Against what everyone else knows is wrong,

Creates soft tissue on a wound that won't heal

Until you repeal.

Your commitment from the Sinners posing as Saints,

Same ones that will put poisonous food on your plate.

Interesting enough I find it,

That amongst people who claim to be spiritually like-minded.

How so much hurt can exist,

Damn right I'm pissed.

Do I revert to the one I was before I got saved?

But I know that's not the road for me that God has paved.

So again, I try to be her armor and her shield,

And do my best to have all her enemies yield.

Takes a lot of work

To recover from the Church Hurt.

Not many are built for it,

The thick skin you need as to God you plead

For an exit and some relief,

As you try to preserve your belief.

In better days coming by way of your anticipated testimony,

To recover from the Church Hurt and expose the religious phonies,

The moment after your failure will be your best one

Because it is YOU that has always been the BLESSED ONE.

Wife my prized possession and secret weapon,

My answer and solution

To Church Hurt and depression,

Was the student ready when the teacher came with this lesson?

Amen

Loving Husband

Richard S. Hunter

Table of Contents

INTRODUCTION

The story you are about to read is my story. At time, even to this day, I reminisce is disbelief as though it was a story, I was reading about someone else. So, at times You will see me switch my perspective from first to second and even to third person. I will do that because at times it still feels so surreal. it's my story and this is how I choose to tell it.

Church hurt at its worst is when you are spiritually broken. That brokenness that your sprit takes on that causes you to be crippled and crushed in your soul. You feel as though you have been smothered and suffocated in a place that should be sacred and full of life. The Devil robbed you in the presence of the Holy Spirit. It's as though you've received spiritual tubal ligation. your soul melted away, disintegrated right out of you, you have felt a decay There is literally a withdrawal from the Holy Spirit. You were rebirthed and blood washed and now you hurt Sunday after Sunday and all week in between, but worse on Sundays while you sit there in pain. Your screams of agony have gone unheard while the repeated crimes against your spirit of burglary and rape continue by an anonymous perpetrator. You try to put on a false face as though trying to endure a failing marriage.

You try to decipher if this bitterness was all you! Or did they cause this? Because you are spiritually dead! You now know that the prevaricators and fornicators that you have dealt with for so long caused this anguish. However, you have discovered through discernment that you are living with **SPIRITBREAKERS!**

You are spiritually unhealthy. Simply put, unhealthy spirits can't occupy the space of the Holy Spirit, who is very much alive. So now you are in your lowest place, you feel worse than you could have ever imagined. You ask God: I*s this Church?* Is this what I'm supposed to feel? How did this happen to me after 20 years of salvation? You barely feel as though you can stand and testify that you have not changed from the godly person God has called you to be! This is my story. My loved ones know I love God. Why did I stay in this place of hurt and humiliation for so long? I was living with a dying spirit. I know my God to be: ALL power, from the one that's Omni-presence, most powerful, worthy to be praised, and worthy of our praises, a strong tower, a wheel in the middle of a wheel, the Prince of peace, the everlasting savior, Yahweh, Jehovah, King of kings, Lord of Lords, deliverer, redeemer, bright and morning star, lily of the valley, lion tribe of Judah, Lamb of God, Alpha and omega, beginning and the end, author and finisher, maker and creator, Mighty ruler, King of glory and the God of my salvation.

I needed an internal revival. I needed to be renewed, restored and refreshed. My spirit had literally been repossessed and I was no longer going to allow that ungodly repo spirit to take what belonged to me!

It was because you Love God, you believe in the Father, Son and the Holy Spirit, you keep showing up and keep coming back. Once again, this is almost like a bad relationship that you stay in far too long, no matter how badly abused you are. The Church can instill spiritual pain, yet some of us will remain, believing God for a change. We stay anticipating that shift to take place. But guess what? God did send you a message. You did not activate what He said. Maybe you did not understand, or you weren't listening in your hearing or you just simply misunderstood.

God speaks and we don't hear. Why? Because you don't have a physical person before you giving you orders. It's easier to understand when someone is physically standing before you.

The spiritual strife in my life was caused by the "holier than thou" type of Christians who don't listen to the Holy Spirit because they think they have all the answers.

CHURCH, I THOUGHT

It was Resurrection Sunday April 16, 2006. This is when I reinstated myself along with my husband joining back at the church in which I grew up and was baptized. Many generations in my family attended there. I was baptized there at age 10 and attended there regularly until I was 20 years of age. I did visit occasionally after that and I had not attended another church on a regular basis. Not to mention both of my children were dedicated as babies there and my daughter was baptized there as well.

What led to this was I also married there on August 13th 2005. "I got me a BOAZ." So, as I begin to visit after the nuptials, I was led to become a member again with my husband by my side. My son at the time as well. My daughter who had just turned 21 the day before had already come back as a member for the last 3 years. She went back as a young adult on her own along with one of my now dearly departed aunts and with my dearly departed grandmother who was of course a pillar and committed member for countless years.

She was there when they constructed a new wing. *Matthew 16:18 And I say also unto thee, that thou art Peter, and upon this rock I will build my church; and the gates of hell shall not prevail against it.* She and many of my family served and built from a little corner small church to a growing in the body of Christ-church, for the community and fellow worshippers. This Baptist church went on to be one of the stellar Baptist churches that the other churches in the area did a lot of fellowship and acknowledged this church as the big sister church throughout the community, locally and far off in regional areas and other boroughs.

Yes, fish fries, chicken dinners, bake and cake sales, raffle selling, bus trips and many other fundraisers and expanding and growing committees and auxiliaries, making disciples and servants. A church evolving and expanding, having different choirs and taking all within them and the power of the Holy Spirit to grow and build this great church that now stands 92 years.

Noticed how earlier I said I was led to be reinstated: QUESTION IS: Was I at that time lead by God? Was I sent there? Or was it a set up?

What I learned in this move is that we must discern and understand God's specific instructions concerning us. God gives clear authorizations in the kingdom and as He speaks, we don't listen. His small whispers are for you to get in your hearing and go when He says go! Move when He says move. Run to or from when He tells you to. The same God that orders our steps is the same God that orders our stops! So, if His answer is no, don't contradict or be contrary to any mighty movement of God. The Lord gives and the Lord takes.

2 Chronicles 16:9 For the eyes of the LORD run to and fro throughout the whole earth, to shew himself strong in the behalf of them whose heart is perfect toward him. Herein thou hast done foolishly: therefore from henceforth thou shalt have wars.

I was in my own spiritual warfare. Right in the church I thought was where I belonged. I was so very wrong. I struggled with whether I was where the Lord and savior my true ALL and ALL; sent me or was I set up originally by the Devil.

MY SPIRITUAL JOURNEY

I knew my ABC's well. I Accepted, Believed and Confessed since 1997. Let me explain. In April of 1996 I was invited to attend my first women's retreat by my dear Aunt. I went to this retreat with my aunt and her church sisters. Oh, this retreat was awesome! When I tell you, I literally and truly received such an amazing breakthrough! I was literally on my face, on my knees, laid out just seeking, receiving every word proclaimed, spoken and preached by these dynamic prophetic anointed women. YES! I learned that weekend. I learned that there is great power.

I knew the Lord but I didn't know the intimately. I knew because hey, I grew up in the church. Until you are born again and receive Christ as your Lord and savior, that you are different, no longer who or what you were; there is a shift and a change in your life. That you now become another person, one with Christ. To Know him and To Know Him and make Him known in your life are two different things. My God the transformation, you have a true metaphoric experience. *2 Corinthians 5:17 Therefore if any man be in Christ, he is a new creature: old things are passed away; behold, all things are become new.*

Fast forward; I would visit and attend this beautiful church with my aunt that I enjoyed the services and the word. It was when one of my dearest, closest, longtime and one of my best friends asked me to come visit her church. We also had another friend who went as well, so I went! NOT ONLY DID I GO!!! I got introduced to the Bible school and this Bishop! My God! I started going Sunday after Sunday and my friend said to me. 'See told you there's a place here for you too!' My kids and I attended and were enjoying it and when I tell you the preaching from this Bishop! My My!

So, since I hadn't joined where I occasionally went with my aunt! There was not only a breakthrough here! BUT this is where I got delivered and saved in one place. That the power of the Holy Spirit became greater than life to me. Life to live daily, life to live freely, life to live acceptingly, life that changed my talk, life that changed my walk, life that changed my thoughts, life that changed my behavior, life that changed how I viewed life, life that changed even how I appeared, life that changed how I looked at others and how I looked at the world, life that became very different in me and within me, life that spoke to me, life that issued my deliverance, life that saved me, life that came alive in me, life that transformed me!

The LIFE OF CHRIST! And I learned one of my favorite scriptures: *Romans 12:1-2 I beseech you therefore, brethren, by the mercies of God, that ye present your bodies a living sacrifice, holy, acceptable unto God, which is your reasonable service. 2 And be not conformed to this world: but be ye transformed by the renewing of your mind, that ye may prove what is that good, and acceptable, and perfect, will of God.*

Although the rest of this scripture is amazing. This is what I got and this is what I learned. This is what I stood on. So now I'm this single mother of 2 and fell in love with the one thing I always had-but did not know I had it. Now that I knew Him, I wanted more of Him. I believed that LOVE was the greatest thing on earth, and as I got saved, I took on an immediate spirit to just love everybody I encountered. I wanted to love them and help them.

There was something about the LOVE of God that gave me an immediate attraction. This introduction came by hearing His Word preached to me by this Illustrious Bishop. Yes, this love was different than the love I had there for my family. This love made me love people in any situation or matter. I wanted to see the world differently. I wanted to see a world without hate, without anger, without the troubles and struggles of the bad and wicked byproducts of sin such as murder, rape, hunger, poverty and lack. There was something about this God. Just as I took on this newfound love and rebirth, I wanted the same for others as well. Because I felt that even all my past wrongs and things that I did was already forgiven. The power in the Holy Spirit is like a sponge that water poured on and I was sucking it up.

Now, during this time, I had also begun at the Bible Institute. When you begin reading His **WORD** and navigating through scriptures, oh what a feeling! The next biggest thing PRAYER... OH MY GOD! Amazing things happen when you develop and begin a prayer life with

God! I studied the theology of prayer. I soon discovered that whether you fall on your knees, stand wherever you are, sitting wherever you are, it doesn't matter. There is something so amazing happening in you and through you that is coming from Him. While I'm praying, He's responding. I was never going to leave this. Not after how it felt! I don't care what you felt after a few times of experiencing sex! I'm just keeping it real. This feeling was the greatest encounter. I hungered for more of His Word, more of His teachings, more of understanding Him as I took a personal oath before Him to serve Him!

I vowed that I wanted and needed Him now in my life forever. Not only for me, but my children, my family and my loved ones. Prayer works. It does changes things! I saw it, I experienced it and I am a witness to it! I knew this was possible and an option for others, absolutely. I started reciting this scripture taught to me by one of my Berean bible instructors in *2 Chronicles 7:14 If my people, which are called by my name, shall humble themselves, and pray, and seek my face, and turn from their wicked ways; then will I hear from heaven, and will forgive their sin, and will heal their land.*

This scripture spoke to me and I felt that it should and could speak to everybody the same. He tells us: just pray, seek Him, and stop what you are doing [the wrongs] This was too good to me. Yes! This God forgives, I just wanted to be one of the people He can count on.

The more I read God's word, the more my thirst grows. Did you know that the bible is an acronym that can stand for **"Basic Instructions Before Leaving Earth?"** So yeah,

I want to take more courses, and did I mention that I joined this great church? Not to any attraction other than the way this awesome Bishop preaches, teaches and would break down this bible. As they say {get in there} I was in there. I attended New Member's classes. I devoured hearing a profound word every Sunday and a powerful bible school. I learned true edification.

I told my friend thank you repeatedly for introducing me to this. This worship experience stayed "off the chain" as they say. We were in watch night services literally every year until like 2am in the morning. So, I am not kidding you. In 1998 I became a member to this great body of Christ. Don't let me leave off the singing now. The growing ministries and the fellowship and I cannot leave out some real true godly people. This was the place to be! This church encapsulated the saying, "Party people in the place to be." Well this was **"praising people in the church to be."** This means service was truly good. I was giving offering but was not yet tithing. That was something that I also began to learn is essential to one who is saved, committed, in a relationship with Christ; that giving is part of our worship experience and that it is an investment in Christ as He already paid it ALL!

The ten percent we as Christians are to give is still not enough – but it's simply the least we can and should do. I am undeniably proud to be a tither in God's kingdom. A mere ten percent to the one who gave His life a ransom for us. YES, he paid the price way back on Calvary, so ten percent can never re-pay or be enough! Being saved we ought to do as the scripture says: *Malachi 3:10 Bring ye all*

*the tithes into the storehouse, that there may be meat in
mine house, and prove me now herewith, saith the LORD of
hosts, if I will not open you the windows of heaven, and
pour you out a blessing, that there shall not be
room enough to receive it.* So, I am truly proud to give and
give exceedingly and abundantly with Jesus joy–He loves a
cheerful giver.

As I previously mentioned, I love the Church I now belong
to and all the good things associated with it such as a stellar
reputation, an awesome worship experience and wonderful
programs put in place from various ministries. We stayed
on fire for Christ and every Sunday and services between
Sundays were a celebration. There was groundbreaking
leadership and growth advancement and potential for
elevation into the kingdom for willing and able bodies that
were true and righteous servants ready and fulfilled to carry
out the assignments attached to their lives.

Let me tell you there was room. Not a room to war with
one another – a room to enlighten and enrich one another.
Not warring but warriors in a kingdom to build and
magnify, exalt and glorify, exhort and edify. This was a
church about our Father's business. This Bishop and
founder were only about His God's business. This was his
vision, his livelihood, and his charge. This Bishop was a
servant by nature, dedicated in heart, and possessed and
believed in his relevance to what God desires of His
people. The Holy Spirit was moving and was using this
Bishop to make disciples. A leader that was defined by
knowing that good leaders go on to make other leaders
great. This church was not growing just in numbers but

growing in discipleship. It was not just members only that joined but vessels willing to serve and commit.

Membership is good but discipleship is better. That church was not just within the walls of this building. But the church was in the body of the people.

UNITY

The bible teaches and speaks of the body of Christ as it relates to the church. So, we shouldn't just go to church we should want to be the church. Some of us actually refer to church as a church home. We go there for mind, body and spiritual healing as the body is a temple. We also attend because we need a WORD from the Lord; as the body of believers it's our servitude.

One Body with Many Members

1 Corinthians 12:12-27 For just as the body is one and has many members, and all the members of the body, though many, are one body, so it is with Christ. 13 For in one Spirit we were all baptized into one body—Jews or Greeks, slaves or free—and all were made to drink of one Spirit.

14 For the body does not consist of one member but of many. 15 If the foot should say, "Because I am not a hand, I do not belong to the body," that would not make it any less a part of the body. 16 And if the ear should say, "Because I am not an eye, I do not belong to the body," that would not make it any less a part of the body. 17 If the whole body were an eye, where would be the sense of hearing? If the whole body were an ear, where would be the sense of smell? *18 But as it is, God arranged the members in the body, each one of them, as he chose. 19 If all were a single member, where would the body be? 20 As it is, there are many parts,[b] yet one body.*

21 The eye cannot say to the hand, "I have no need of you," nor again the head to the feet, "I have no need of you." 22 On the contrary, the parts of the body that seem to be weaker are indispensable, 23 and on those parts of the body that we think less honorable we bestow the greater honor, and our unpresentable parts are treated with greater modesty, 24 which our more presentable parts do not require. But God has so composed the body, giving greater honor to the part that lacked it, 25 that there may be no division in the body, but that the members may have the same care for one another. 26 If one member suffers, all suffer together; if one member is honored, all rejoice together.

27 Now you are the body of Christ and individually members of it.

We make our way into the house of the Lord to worship in His presence with others that are of the same faith. Fellowship brings joy, happiness, peace and solace. There's something in the atmosphere that when we all get together in worship that comes upon us as when they all were on the day of Pentecost: ***Acts 2:1-21*** *The Coming of the Holy Spirit When the day of Pentecost arrived, they were all together in one place. 2 And suddenly there came from heaven a sound like a mighty rushing wind, and it filled the entire house where they were sitting. 3 And divided tongues as of fire appeared to them and rested[a] on each one of them. 4 And they were all filled with the Holy Spirit* *and began to speak in other tongues as the Spirit gave them utterance.*

See, to me, and to many others coming into the church is the next best greatest thing to serving God. When you become a born-again Christian, you are auctioned by the Holy Spirit. Your new nature is to operate, function and carry yourself in such a way that Church becomes second nature. With every fiber of our being we are told, *"for in Him we live and move and have our being, as also some of your own poets have said, 'For we are also His offspring."* **Acts 17:28,** we are designed to want to run into the house of worship-simply go to church. Our haven, our reinforced attitudes and this engages us so that we make it day by day based on what we hear and what we're told and what we understand. My entering would feel like I'm some outlet and the right extension just plugged into me. This got me through, it carried me through, and it served my hearts yearning and desire for God. I was a teachable being. But how did I suddenly become unreachable by this church? That hurt!

My eagerness slipped away because of this unspeakable pain! Shame and ungodly humiliation. No one knew how hurt I truly felt even as it progressed and got worse, not even my husband. I literally came to a place where I lived with this ripping, crippling, eating away and destroying me. I was crushed. My inner spirit was a believer but what happened? How did I self-destruct? Is the devil taking advantage? How did I become vulnerable in Satan's kingdom? Was I weak? I don't think so? Did I allow this temple, me as a vessel to fall prey? Huh? The devil resides in me? Lord help, this is a lie from the pit of Hell! I was suffering in silence. I became a castaway. I want to share something. If you ever feel yourself slipping away in sadness, drowning in sorrow, feeling pitiful to your stomach like oppression and depression are creeping up; be mindful, be cautious, be careful and get the help and the counseling that you need. DON'T BE embarrassed, ashamed or have concerns of what others will think or say. Be concerned with oneself as God has concern regarding us:

Psalm 138:8 (NLT) The LORD will work out his plans for my life—for your faithful love, O LORD, endures forever. Don't abandon me, for you made me.

So please note that God cares and has concern for His people. I was swallowed in the devil's trap! Be aware that Satan is clever, he's practical, tactical and is strategic on all fronts. Let me point this out. Although the devil himself may not be using you! He does use other people to get to you! Those are the ones vulnerable and weak. The Devil keeps his way with them in season and out! He no longer needs to attack them because they are already attached to the secular lifestyle. He got into the rhythm of their life and they walk with him, run with him, dance with him and move with him; they even sit with him. He took control and to their dis-advantage they began to run amuck, reap havoc, tear down, cast out, destroy, destruct, ruin things and they just become the executors of mess. They are master-trouble makers and never peacemakers; problem creators and never problem solvers. These satanic instruments always cause division never any harmony and they enlist separation never inseparability. These instruments of the enemy disrupt unity and oneness. Paul calls for oneness.

1 Corinthians 1:10 I appeal [beseech/exhort/urge] to you, dear brothers and sisters, by the authority of our Lord Jesus Christ, to live in harmony with each other. Let there be no divisions in the church. Rather, be of one mind, united [joined/knit together] in thought and purpose [conviction/same judgment].

And please be aware that it does not stop there! The scriptures are replete with the instructions, teachings and the doctrine of us being on one accord, joined together, bonded in one spirit, complete in UNITY! Paul admonishes and repeatedly speaks of it:

Romans 1:13
I do not want you to be unaware, brothers, how often I planned to come to you (but have been prevented from visiting until now), in order that I might have a harvest among you, just as I have had among the other Gentiles.

1 Corinthians 3:3
for you are still worldly. For since there is jealousy and dissension among you, are you not worldly? Are you not walking in the way of man?

1 Corinthians 11:18
First of all, I hear that when you come together as a church, there are divisions among you, and in part I believe it.

2 Corinthians 13:11
Finally, brothers, rejoice! Aim for perfect harmony, encourage one another, be of one mind, live in peace. And the God of love and peace will be with you.

2 Thessalonians 2:1
Now we beseech you, brethren, by the coming of our Lord Jesus Christ, and by our gathering together unto him,

Philippians 1:27
Nevertheless, conduct yourselves in a manner worthy of the gospel of Christ. Then, whether I come and see you or hear about you in my absence, I will know that you stand firm in one spirit, contending side by side for the faith of the gospel,

Then Peter speaks of it:

1 Peter 5:10
And after you have suffered for a little while, the God of all grace, who has called you to His eternal glory in Christ, will Himself restore you, secure you, strengthen you, and establish you.

It's in the Psalms even:

Psalm133:1
A Song of degrees of David. Behold, how good and how pleasant it is for brethren to dwell together in unity!

Jeremiah talks of it:

Jeremiah32:39
And I will give them one heart, and one way that they may fear me forever, for the good of them, and of their children after them:

John mentions it:

John 13:34,35
A new commandment I give unto you, That ye love one
another; as I have loved you, that ye also love one another

There must be UNITY in the body of Christ!!! There must
be a connection in the Kingdom! There must be a divine
intervention for the saints to break bread together, come
together, love on one another, build together, uplift,
enlighten and encourage one another. If we do not inspire
each other we just die with each other – in an ungodly,
unfulfilled purpose without real peace; instead, just in
pieces. True saints have an obligation when we belong to a
congregation! Praise and worship is for the purpose of
ALL! Please make note: The Holy Spirit is not prejudice
(He's for everybody and anybody-He's for ALL). That's
why we gather! Not independently, not individually or for
one's benefit or one's self pleasure. We are to be
compelled and unparalleled so that there is an alignment
with the order of God! Unity is not personal. Look how
the:

Appeal to Unity

1 Corinthians 1-16 *Amplified Bible (AMP)*
1 Paul, called as an apostle (special messenger, personally
chosen representative) of Jesus Christ by the will of God,
and our brother Sosthenes,

2 To the church of God in Corinth, to those sanctified (set
apart, made holy) in Christ Jesus, who are
selected and called as saints (God's people), together with

all those who in every place call on and honor the name of our Lord Jesus Christ, their Lord and ours:

3 Grace to you and peace [inner calm and spiritual well-being] from God our Father and the Lord Jesus Christ.

4 I thank my God always for you because of the grace of God which was given you in Christ Jesus, 5 so that in everything you were [exceedingly] enriched in Him, in all speech [empowered by the spiritual gifts] and in all knowledge [with insight into the faith]. 6 In this way our testimony about Christ was confirmed and established in you, 7 so that you are not lacking in any spiritual gift [which comes from the Holy Spirit], as you eagerly await [with confident trust] for the revelation of our Lord Jesus Christ [when He returns]. 8 And He will also confirm you to the end [keeping you strong and free of any accusation, so that you will be] blameless and beyond reproach in the day [of the return] of our Lord Jesus Christ. 9 God is faithful [He is reliable, trustworthy and ever true to His promise— He can be depended on], and through Him you were called into fellowship with His Son, Jesus Christ our Lord.

10 But I urge you, believers, by the name of our Lord Jesus Christ, that all of you be in full agreement in what you say, and that there be no divisions or factions among you, but that you be perfectly united in your way of thinking and in your judgment [about matters of the faith]. 11 For I have been informed about you, my brothers and sisters, by those of Chloe's household, that there are quarrels and factions among you. 12 Now I mean this, that each one of you says, "I am [a disciple] of Paul," or "I am [a disciple] of Apollos," or "I am [a disciple] of Cephas (Peter)," or "I am [a disciple] of Christ." 13 Has Christ been divided [into different parts]?

Was Paul crucified for you? Or were you baptized into the name of Paul? [Certainly not!] 14 I thank God that I did not baptize any of you except Crispus and Gaius, 15 so that no one would say that you were baptized into my name. 16 Now I also baptized the household of Stephanas; beyond that, I do not know if I baptized anyone else. 17 For Christ did not send me [as an apostle] to baptize, but [commissioned and empowered me] to preach the good news [of salvation]— not with clever and eloquent speech [as an orator], so that the cross of Christ would not be [b]made ineffective [deprived of its saving power].

Paul was "**called** to be an apostle of Jesus Christ through the will of God..." *(1 Cor. 1:1)*. He was an apostle chosen to do the kind of work he was doing.

*For all things are yours, whether **Paul**, or Apollos, or Cephas, or the world, or life, or death, or things present, or things to come; for all are yours;*

*2 **Timothy** 2:22 Flee the evil desires of youth and pursue righteousness, faith, love and peace, along with those who call on the Lord out of a pure heart.*

Paul's doctrine in the New Testament is a revelation of the Old Testament. He teaches and he pleads to us of God's wisdom, His ways, His works and His will. These are for us to exercise even now, more than ever. Our sin nature is much deeper than skin. Understanding unity helps us to conform to how we should behave as a body of believers. For therein lies our progression and growth, as we are told

If there is a natural body, there is also a spiritual body. So, given that we are all spiritual beings in our natural bodies. Combined, equipped and designed to operate together. Remember we are told in **Romans 8:11,** *But if the Spirit of him that raised up Jesus from the dead dwell in you, he that raised up Christ from the dead shall also quicken your mortal bodies by his Spirit that dwelleth in you.*

So that alone is enough to have every one of us functioning under that wonderful umbrella of UNITY! That great big banner that we all raise should govern our behaviors as reflected by Christ on Calvary. The cross is the gospel. The cross signifies a rallying point for all God's people to assemble as called for by God.

FAITH

It is God's purpose for all believer's to "attain the unity of the faith." With many Christians, and especially with evangelicals, there has been a tendency to confuse **faith** and **doctrine**. We need to recognize those who are truly accepted by the Lord. Faith is not doctrine, but obedience to the Lord... It is through faith that we are saved, and not by correct teaching.

Ephesians 2:8 For it is by grace you have been saved, through faith—and this is not from yourselves, it is the gift of God—James 1:22-25 Do not merely listen to the word, and so deceive yourselves. Do what it says. 23 Anyone who listens to the word but does not do what it says is like someone who looks at his face in a mirror 24 and, after looking at himself, goes away and immediately forgets what he looks like. 25 But whoever looks intently into the perfect law that gives freedom, and continues in it—not forgetting what they have heard, but doing it—they will be blessed in what they do. James 2:14-26 What good is it, my brothers and sisters, if someone claims to have faith but has no deeds? Can such faith save them? 15 Suppose a brother or a sister is without clothes and daily food. 16 If one of you says *to them, "Go in peace; keep warm and well fed," but does nothing about their physical needs, what good is it?* 17 *In the same way, faith by itself, if it is not accompanied by action, is dead.* 18 *But someone will say, "You have faith; I have deeds.* "Show me your faith without deeds, and I will show you my faith by my deeds.* 19 *You believe that there is one God. Good! Even the demons believe that—and shudder.* 20 *You foolish person, do you want evidence that faith without deeds is useless[a]?* 21 *Was not our father Abraham considered righteous for what he did when he offered his son Isaac on the altar?* 22 *You see that his faith and his actions were working together, and his faith was made complete by what he did.* 23 *And the scripture was fulfilled that says, "Abraham believed God, and it was credited to him as righteousness,"[b] and he was called God's friend.* 24 *You see that a person is considered righteous by what they do and not by faith alone.* 25 *In the same way, was not even Rahab the prostitute considered righteous for what she did when she gave lodging to the spies and sent them off in a different direction?* 26 *As the body without the spirit is dead, so faith without deeds is dead.*

Understanding saving grace, Paul explained it: That it is the Christian's first motivation for living a godly life. Unity is essential in our faith. We believe, we grow, and we mature. Even our faith must not be contrary to the Word of God – but be a replication of God's Word! We must model Him by faith in action. Faith works! Faith to believe! Faith to receive! Faith in God sends the message that we trust Him, we magnify Him, we adore Him, also honor Him, we celebrate Him, we give Him an encore, we serve Him, we know Him and in our inner faith we are letting Him know this and our outward expression makes Him known to the world around us. There's an art we must master in exercising our faith. To allow that power of God to direct our hearts and mind. There's faith in our souls. Do you truly know what it is to have strong faith? *Matthew 17:20 And Jesus said unto them, Because of your unbelief: for verily I say unto you, If ye have faith as a grain of mustard seed, ye shall say unto this mountain, Remove hence to yonder place; and it shall remove; and nothing shall be impossible unto you.*

Faith is told in *Hebrews 11:1 Now faith is the substance of things hoped for, the evidence of things not seen.*

Faith is assurance of the things hoped for, expected, expectancy, clarity, definite, claimed and received. Faith is also the conviction of things not seen. So, we conclude it before it even comes to pass. Already not accepted, it's like knowing its dead, not even coming to us, never even claimed. Understand we are saying that we have objection and not rejection! That we have something objective rather than subjective. The specific illustration of the definition of faith is EVIDENCE! I believe God is the maker and creator of the world and everything! So, I understand, that in my conviction of this I am convinced. The evidence of faith where God's invisible attributes are said to be "clearly seen" by man, namely, *Romans 1:20 Since the creation of the world [God's] invisible attributes, his eternal power and divine nature, have been clearly seen, being understood by what has been made. so that people are without excuse.* The word "understood" here is the same word as in *Hebrews 11:3 By faith we understand that the universe was formed at God's command, so that what is seen was not made out of what was visible.*

Having strong faith is a learned attribute we must have. You can't just say you have faith without an understanding of what it is you have FAITH in. Faith without works is dead. Please note: Your faith can and will be put to a test! It becomes your story, your truth, your testimony. Why because you still have and own up to the faith indwelled and instilled inside of you. Faith challenges you – but you remain focus. Your belief outweighs your burdens, you trust in Him supersedes the troubles. Your purpose is driven by God, so the problems aren't as big. His divine presence stops the distractions; your faith remains in your actions and nothing and no one can falsify that! Faith is our foundation for believers.

SPIRITUALLY RAPED

This is a strong phrase, right? It is true though. I was spiritually raped. I was a victim. I experienced this. I went through this. I witnessed it repeatedly happening to me. Why because I was worth more than I received. I was a godly woman, a woman of God! I'm not boasting or bragging or claiming to be something that I wasn't. I understand what you are thinking, what you are you saying? How can she think she's really all of that and be Ms. Holier than thou? That's not what I'm saying. I am saying that I went through the most awful experience in a church than any Christian should have ever experienced.

I am not talking about a bad relationship, marriage, engaged, girlfriend, boyfriend, or partnership.

I am not talking about a working on a bad job that just wasn't no good and yet you stayed.

I am not talking about a poor relationship between parent and child, mother, daughter, father or son.

I am not talking a stepparent, stepsister or stepbrother not getting along.

I am not talking about physical abuse.

I am not talking about a bad drug habit, alcohol abuse, or even illicit drug use.

I am not talking a pimp/prostitute relationship gone wrong.

I am not talking about a child abuse situation, physical or sexual.

I am not talking mental abuse, controlling of someone.

I am not talking about sexually raped.

I am talking about EXACTLY what I said! Spiritually raped; YES! In "The Church."

Unheard of, maybe! But is it possible? Absolutely – WHY? Because it happened to me.

It started September 2011 when I was asked to speak for the 1st time on a pre-women's day program. However, at that time I never knew; rather I had no idea there was a spiritual attack on my life. Or should I say a spiritual attack in the making. Because it did not fully come to light until the very next year in September of 2012 when I was asked again to speak and do the closing at the pre-women's program for that year. I was asked by one of the two that asked the prior year and the other person agreed but with stipulations regarding me speaking and 'NOT PREACHING'. With all the women and even the men being all excited and talking about it and saying how she's going to take us home again, many people telling me they can't wait. How all my family and friends were looking so forward to coming out again. I was taken by the outpouring of love and compliments. I was overjoyed and yet excited about the WORD of God and yes, I had a Word from the Lord. One thing stuck out though. It was the year before on the Sunday after the Friday night's worship that I received such a wonderful compliment from my pastor-but that day and that day only.

Well, fast forward to 2012. We have a meeting with the chairs and the committee relating to the upcoming event. I WAS BLOWN AWAY! I was pretty much railroaded into being told that my paper was a sermon. I'm only supposed to speak and who asked me to preach. And the co-chair stated that's why we wanted her to close us out again. The chair advised me to rewrite and shorten it to less than five minutes. The Co-chair verbally said we agreed to let her do seven so that it goes off well she has a Word to deliver. Final answer no! I was advised after I corrected it to bring it back for review. I'm an obedient person to those in charge, so I did just that. I now realized I had a target on my back. I was led to feel that I was lied to, for the sake of some unknown politics. I then gave the revised and she approved.

As a result of the committee's nonsense, I told my family not to attend the Friday night's service. It was hard to restrain myself and dilute the power God placed in me to use within those four heavily edited minutes. I felt like Jeremiah when he said, "it's like fire shut up in my bones." I was told to just speak. They cut and took so much from my message that I stood before His people afraid because of the demands put on me. They're in charge. Ironically, the person before me which was the thorn in my side at the time spoke almost 10 minutes. Meanwhile, at the meeting they said they were speaking less than five minutes because they're obedient. This woman was the biggest Jezebel you have ever met. She was defiant, deceitful, disruptive, disturbing and distrusting. Still defying God's truth as they did the great prophets Elijah and Elisha. *1 Kings 21:23 And of Jezebel the LORD also said, 'The dogs shall eat Jezebel within the walls of Jezreel.'*

Also be careful and aware how the spirit of Jezebel seeks to manipulate others who you never had a problem with. In my case I was close, adored and was rather fond of the other person in charge of the service. We came from the same church in the past, we served on a community choir together and had outstanding times in fellowship. So, the actions came out of nowhere suddenly and abruptly. BUT I understand the dynamics of when you have newfound kingdom friends so to speak. Spirits can be very strong and dominating! You have to recognize and be aware that it has a domino effect!

As for me I had to remember *Psalm 34:18 The LORD is close to the brokenhearted and saves those who are crushed in spirit.*

And although we are a year later. The big question remained from last year when so many asked "What did your pastor say?" My answer was always the same. He made one comment to me privately Sunday during the meet and greet time and said, "you did a wonderful job!"

I continued going to church serving and being glad that the members enjoyed it. All the efforts I contributed were appreciated and it turned out to be a wonderful event. They were hoping for many more. It is hard however to move forward in unity when you have to stifle your anointing for the sake of demonic agendas.

My takeaway from this is that the evil of the few did not outweigh the good of the many. I must say that I loved the members and congregation. Oh, how I love them! They were not my enemies; they were not never, or did they ever target me. My God; I could not really begin to explain how the support from them was endless. From the start, the beginning and always. They loved on me as the body of Christ calls us to. That we were overjoyed and loved being with one another in worship and all the church functions and affairs throughout the different committees, ministries and auxiliaries. Just all God. Always exciting and wonderful. How they forever stayed encouraging me, enlightening me and pushing me, believing that there was more in me and more for me. The overwhelming joy and support of almost the entire church body is countless. Who can ask for more!

It was because of them that I stayed and remained as long as I did. My experience with such love and unity was likened to the upper room experience. I just loved them all to life... *Acts 1:12-14 Then they returned to Jerusalem from the mount called Olivet, which is near Jerusalem, a Sabbath day's journey. 13 And when they had entered, they went up into the upper room where they were staying: Peter, James, John, and Andrew; Philip and Thomas; Bartholomew and Matthew; James the son of Alphaeus and Simon the Zealot; and Judas the son of James. These all continued with one [a]accord in prayer and supplication, with the women and Mary the mother of Jesus, and with His brothers.*

We were saints serving while we prayed. Believing God. I learned to watch the few enemies I had. I just let my enemies be my footstool. I didn't walk over them; I certainly wasn't walking with them! I just learned to walk around them. We were not like minded.

It didn't just stop there. By God's grace and discernment, I learned how to contend with those who did not like me but pretended to. The next few years got progressively worse. Leaving was not a case of my lack of faith in my God, my case went deeper than that. The mess I saw and witnessed not to mention things I knew that others didn't would even confuse the devil. Simply put, "The Church" can hurt and make you feel spiritually raped!

In the next chapter you will hear about how I went through true kingdom humiliation.

KINGDOM HUMILIATION
Part 1

First, how do you fix or repair humiliation after it's done, and the effects are on the outside? The answer is, it's difficult. It's simply a different level to face this type of ungodly humiliation emulating from the house of God. This is supposed to be a place you go for a fresh word, a worship experience, peace, serenity and comfort. I know the building inside the four walls is not the church BUT the people in there make up the church. As in *Matthew 16:18-19 And I say also unto thee, That thou art Peter, and upon this rock I will build my church; and the gates of hell shall not prevail against it. 19 And I will give unto thee the keys of the kingdom of heaven: and whatsoever thou shalt bind on earth shall be bound in heaven: and whatsoever thou shalt loose on earth shall be loosed in heaven.*

We are there to build expand and grow God's kingdom; Well, at least some of us. Believe me, tearing down strongholds is real! You must know that not everybody who shows up is there to worship. But instead showing up for the worst they can offer. Please make a mental note the Devil is not showing up in a long red cape, pitchfork in hand and horns on his head. But showing up in the flesh looking like the rest of us just covered in mess and looking to destroy everybody else's life. It's frightening to know that these people are not convicted felons walking the streets but unexposed and unrepented wolves in sheep's clothing who are sitting in the pews among us. To say that they are playing church is an understatement. Church to me was becoming one big church masquerade ball with a hand full wearing the devil's mask. Thank God it wasn't more than a hand full, because the truth is had it been any more, I would have been dead! Not figuratively I do mean literally. You will understand later.

Let me bring to your attention how they can preach, and they can teach! But *Matthew 15:7-10 You hypocrites! Isaiah was right when he prophesied about you:*
8 " 'These people honor me with their lips,
    but their hearts are far from me.
9 They worship me in vain;
    their teachings are merely human rules.' "
10 Jesus called the crowd to him and said, "Listen and understand.

That was it! God's truth has and always will be truth. Words to live by. As He said Listen and understand. Don't you know He knew this? That's why He makes it clear so you understand who you are listening too. In fact, know who you are listening to in your hearing. "Listen and understand" go hand in hand with watch and pray – 'Pray and watch'.

You just can't make this stuff up. It's real, it's truth and it's fact, especially in my life. I know the Devil is the father of lies, when my God is the Father of truth.

The humiliation was during the period between 2016 through 2018. Let me start at the beginning. In November of 2015, the woman who raised me, my grandmother who I called Mama, took sick. Well I had been in school at my church since January of that year. This school was introduced to the congregation by "persons in charge". Let me mention that when I originally returned in 2006, I held the certificate of Evangelist. So anyway, moving along it's now December, Mama was in the hospital a month. Part of my course requirement was to be a part of Saturday morning platform at church that involved two of us speaking. This was my second time that year. After class I was approached by the person, I put too much trust, belief and faith in so of course being approached I was elated. A yes moment! You know God answers prayers so I'm just besides myself and glad to glory and ALL that! Why? Because I was told we would meet and move on to ministry from there!

Oh! You can't just tell someone like me, who is so excited about ministry just anything without me taking it to heart. I would do anything for the glory of the Lord. My family and husband were thrilled for me. My husband was especially excited for me because he knew I wanted this. I was naming and claiming it and calling it and receiving it. ALL that! Always remember that your calling is from God and should never be placed in man's hand. Otherwise man will disappoint, so be prepared.

1 thought this was a great way to start off the New Year! That my meeting was to take place in January. I was still attending Berean Bible Institute since that September; I was currently in two schools. (Well, Mama passed that January 1st 2016). I must share what happened to me on that first Sunday in December 2015 after my good news was received that Saturday; I had left church that Sunday. I took my granddaughter to a kids Birthday party. And I couldn't stay because there was this sense of urgency to get to the hospital and see Mama and that came out of know where! So of course, the human side of me was, "oh God please don't tell me Mama took a turn." I just couldn't explain this feeling I never felt or encountered when I lost close loved ones in the past my grandfather, my uncle, my brother, my aunt I mean really close, their passing's were very difficult.

BUT as I got to the hospital my granddaughter and I went into the room no other family was there which was unusual for a late Sunday afternoon, strange ... But what was the strangest was my new encounter with The Master; Oh, my true God! There was a spiritual exchange and the way the Lord was talking to me I had never experienced this. It was different from my transformation when I became saved and delivered that it was almost to a feeling of, "God is this for me and to me?" What is happening? I have my grandbaby with me and Mama raised up from the side of the bed turned and sat up and started talking and speaking telling me, "you go ahead and preach", she knew pastor was going to say something to me and all this stuff, meanwhile she was laying there almost in a coma.

The CNA and nurses said she wouldn't move or talk or anything. She wouldn't eat she let me and my grandbaby both feed her. It's just there was a different aura in the atmosphere. The room CNA never saw me before and asked, are you a minister? out of the blue and there was nothing to make her say what transpired in the room since I arrived. I had not even prayed with Mama yet and when I did, the other three patients in the room and their families all of a sudden became silent.

I've prayed in hospitals and places a thousand times and I don't know what was different this time. Somewhere deep inside I knew that the Lord was preparing me for the event of someday mama going from labor to reward. Do you know since she got sick and has been in the hospital, I was sick to my stomach, not eating, stress, praying and worried? Well, I got a testimony, God lifted it that day. I left with a different feeling than I came with. I came there in hurt pieces and left with a newfound peace. I took my grandbaby home. I couldn't share or tell nobody, other than the one call I made from the hospital. I called my dear friend and sister in Christ. She was someone I adored and was fond of. She understood the entire concept and helped to enlighten me further. I received what she said, I accepted what God did, and it was done. I will share later another testimony about Mama – but I need to move on with my kingdom humiliation.

The meeting that was to take place didn't because Mama passed January 1, 2016. So, the 1st meeting was March 2016. All went well and I was told how we need to get on the fast track. My regret was Mama would not be here to see this! Just a wonderful discussion which my husband was present. There was one brief interruption from someone who needed a quick word of prayer so the four of us gathered around for a quick prayer, then the person left, and we proceeded and closed with a well accomplished journey, so I thought!

The follow-up meeting took place in April 2016. I went in one way and came out another. It was like I met with another person, the things that we were to be following up on was no longer the agenda, but now we're on the road to this delay. In my mind I was trying to discern the reason for this new delay and what came to me was **James 1:8** A double minded man is unstable in all his ways. The bible even speaks how even godly men sometimes lapse into double **mindedness**. That was my sign, the clue was right there. I know how the meeting last month that was interrupted by a particular person had everything under the sun to do with this ungodly twist [sadly for me I wish it was under the Son of God, it would have been different]. I left feeling cast downed and spiritually destroyed. I laid in bed that night with tears in my eyes because I was dismayed and just walked away with the only thing, I could say to myself. I said, "that's the pastor, it's his church and he can do what he wants, the Lord will make a way out of no way." I have to except my nay like my yay and my no like yes. Pray, keep it moving get past it-I won't be the first or the last to have this happen. I had to remind myself of **Jeremiah 29:11** *For I know the plans I have for you," declares the* LORD, *"plans to prosper you and not to harm you, plans to give you hope and a future.* Well, I knew my destiny was just dynamite that went off for NOW! But not for always because someone else just lit that stick of dynamite… I had to be reminded of the faith I claim to have. I'm not about to fail in faith NOW!

Well I continued doing me so to speak. I admit I had some wrong in my actions because I then began to show up in service and not praise and worship and clap and shout. {Who the HELL are you}? It wasn't in my nature or my character to behave like this. BUT I only did it intently when that person was present. NOTE: Be careful about the fact that the Devil is cleaver and he can play with your emotions and challenge you to commit and be spiteful and deceitful. BUT as prayer warriors and God-fearing Christians, don't let no Devil in HELL steal your joy. The World didn't give you your joy and the world can't take it away. But I was of flesh! Angry and hurt. "Shake it off and get on sistah!", is what I repeatedly told myself. Now you coming in the sanctuary with a level of praise because of all the other stuff you got going on and knowing how good God is and you see "them" and it suddenly halts? How can you let the Devil rob you? YES! Well, news flash you better go and take it back! Give him a pass for the temporary taking. Declaring he will never get it again!!! This is hard truth.

I told myself these things, but I was regurgitating and laying in my own vomit. Threw it up and stayed in it. The worst kind of wound is the self-inflicted one. The body of Christ has a way of inflicting its own hurt as the enemy sits in the front row with a bag of popcorn. He watches and he gets the screen credit for somethings that we chose to do to ourselves by ourselves. The hurt, human Christian humiliation. I don't care how many scriptures I knew, how much I loved Jesus, how I just loved people and the caring compassionate person I was and had been since I was reborn. This was the fight of my life. The life I wanted to have in Christ. I was in Christ, but I needed more. I wanted more of Him, I desired Him, I desired this. Yeah, I wanted to preach to the hurt, the hungry, the lost and broken but I couldn't even help myself right about now. I was weak and crippled. This is what I heard my inner voice saying to me.

I was the hardest rock crying out to rock of my salvation, the rock of all ages, my rock, sword and shield. Crying was an understatement. I was screaming. I would get in my car and head into work in the mornings and it felt as though every car could hear me crying out on the Cross-Island parkway in New York.

A month went by I was approached by someone very special and not with my permission, but they said something to the person large and in charge! They didn't like it. Would you believe this person in had the audacity to go and say to my husband **'your wife is skating on thin ice!'** Yup you heard me. Well praise be to God it was said to him because only the Lord knows, had it been said directly to me, well we won't go there. I wasn't always saved, but by the grace of God. I thank him that I am and also that it wasn't said to a few family men I know. See my husband is saved on a whole different level. Even some of you reading this right now saying what: he still breathing. [*What did my husband do or say back to him*]? Well what my husband did not know is that those words were not an idol threat. He was in a position of authority and he intended on seeing this threat to fruition.

And yes, it troubled my husband, so a month later they went out to 'break bread' so to speak and fix this. Make up, correct, do over/start over, whatever the case. Well since part of my character is a people pleaser, we ended revisiting the situation all over again. My husband currently is the Chairman of the Trustee Board. Who took his position seriously and wanted to see me happy! We agreed to a meeting. I'm a forgiving person it took place July 20, 2016. But I should have took Paul's advice that there are some out there that invent their own gospel. Except this invention was created by him and someone else! You know how false ministers-a form of godliness: Paul said it. These false doctrines deny the power of God. Sent by themselves not sent by God. I'm sorry and I know I sound bitter - but the truth is it made me better. Paul warns, "Have nothing to do with them." *2 Timothy 3:5-8* *having a form of godliness but denying its power. Have nothing to do with such people. 6 For among them are those who creep into households and capture weak women, burdened with sins and led astray by various passions, 7 always learning and never able to arrive at a knowledge of the truth. 8 Just as Jannes and Jambres opposed Moses, so these men also oppose the truth, men corrupted in mind and disqualified regarding the faith.*

That meeting got us nowhere. Not worth the time I need to give to my good God. I'm on God's time and I literally just wasted it with the Devil in disguise. Preparation time is never supposed to be wasted time.

I am having trouble trying to figure out how is this possible for people to do an imitation of the gospel without truly imitating a true GOD! What am I missing?

In the meantime, some great things were happening in my life. Before the next planned meeting I graduated as the Salutatorian on June 5th, 2016 and gave the commencement address. The theme was Anointed to Win. Well, when I tell you as I said I love the people. They came out in numbers and supported me the congregants from the seniors on down! Truth I did not expect the turn out myself. This was an overwhelming surprise at 6pm on a Sunday evening. But the Lord does say:

Isaiah 26:3 (AMP) "You will keep in perfect and constant peace the one whose mind is steadfast [that is, committed and focused on You—in both [b]inclination and character], Because he trusts and takes refuge in You [with hope and confident expectation].

1 Peter 5:7 (AMP) casting all your cares [all your anxieties, all your worries, and all your concerns, once and for all] on Him, for He cares about you [with deepest affection, and watches over you very carefully].

Nahum 1:7 (AMP)The LORD is good,
A strength and stronghold in the day of trouble;
He knows [He recognizes, cares for, and understands fully] those who take refuge and trust in Him.

No need to mention who was not there-because they never are for anything concerning me whenever or wherever I preached. Now the other person was there, why? As part of the graduating class we both belonged to the same school. I just was there much longer of course but there are some things that it's not what you know or how much you know- It's who you know! Well know this – I KNOW GOD!

Imagine the theme: *Anointed to Win* – when you feel like you are completely losing! Well, I stood as I always stand before God's people, I stood with power, purpose and conviction. I am an advocate for Christ. A servant first. My **problems can't outweigh my purpose**. Because in fact, I was only losing to man NOT to God! We must not expect validation from man but allow God to validate us. He is the orchestrator and the dictator. I got complacent over a piece of paper. Don't you know that with or without that paper you are a servant. Never hold a title in your life that will stand between you and our master. The Bible says: God is no respecter of person.

Matthew 25:21 His lord/master said unto him, Well done, thou good and faithful servant: thou hast been faithful over a few things, I will make thee ruler over many things: enter thou into the joy/happiness of thy lord.. Don't be left down here fighting for a piece of paper. I know credentials are important and they do help you to accelerate in life with open doors; but not at the expense of letting Godly opportunities shut on you spiritually. Even when I'm writing I feel like preaching… Help me Holy Spirit!

Understand, I was truly honored and I could not explain the happiness and privilege to have been given this wonderful opportunity. And to top it off having the unnumbered support and backing of a church that saw the true God in me. Yes, the God in me but they didn't see the hurt in me! So, might I add that the July meeting, no mention was made of this great event. Just like nothing else I accomplished was given any attention. Silly me to think anything different.

Yes, to be HURT beyond some degree. There was a time I was doing a lot that, others recognized it and thought that I would be licensed and elevated. The people in my church, my family, my friends, neighbors, and on my job. Just repeatedly and literally asking all the time. When are you getting your ministerial credentials as you already operate in that capacity? The asking and inquiring became frustrating to hear! As I knew it was not going to happen considering whom I was under. They did not know that someone had performed a spiritual hysterectomy on me. That at times I felt like saying shut the hell up. As it was adding to my betrayal, hurt and embarrassment, the downfall and the letdown. I realized that they cared and loved me as I loved them, and only had my best interest at heart as they knew the WORD of the Lord was embedded in me. However, I found myself no longer appreciating the asking because it became a hurtful feeling.

Matthew 7:21-23 True and False Disciples
21 "Not everyone who says to me, 'Lord, Lord,' will enter the kingdom of heaven, but only the one who does the will of my Father who is in heaven. 22 Many will say to me on that day, 'Lord, Lord, did we not prophesy in your name and in your name drive out demons and in your name perform many miracles?' 23 Then I will tell them plainly, 'I never knew you. Away from me, you evildoers!

Part 2

The Church soap opera continues, this church drama goes on, this menace in ministry is real! As this mess turns. Before I tell you the next phase of problems, I need to share what thus saith the Lord! We invent and make problems God is not pleased, we destroy our brothers and sisters to the core and that we want to have titles and belong to the fivefold ministry *Ephesians 4:11 And he gave some, apostles; and some, prophets; and some, evangelists; and some, pastors and teachers.*

This was Christ himself who gave. So how is it that those who claim to be called by God make such a mockery of His anointing. Although the world didn't give it and the world can't take it away; we should learn not grieve the Holy Spirit with our antics and our carnal attempts to manipulate through the anointing. It's also not ok to play favorites in the church. You can't let your authority and power in title only devour God's people.

You cannot allow cliques to infiltrate on God's property. The church is now in danger. The flock is leaving. I'm personally seeing church membership drop. The hurtful thing is we are also losing disciples not just church members. But because of the actions and the nature of dooms day church you're not making disciples when you are creating devils. The synagogue of Satan has caused catastrophe to the church. The demons have caused demolition. We are seeing the church body disrupted by filth and unclean spirits. God has never called for this, He never ordained this. Its man's stained and tainted nature.

The spirit of Christ will not be upset or disturbed by these actions because we ALL know that the wrath of God. He brings correction. He made himself clear in *1 Samuel* when Eli's house was cut off. So, continue to think this disobedience will go on unpaid. The day of reckoning will come before further wreck is done.

I don't believe you are called when you're just picked at the hand of man and not at the hand of God-by man. You are not called when you're appointed and there's no anointing, you are not called just because you're someone's favorite. Favoritism is not the favor of God. You can be chosen by man and still frozen in time by God. There becomes a time when you must realize if you're in this position, there's a part of your heart that still needs thawing out, you got some defrosting, yet to take place. You're not prepared, you still got stuff in you that needs to be purified. You need to be cleansed. You're not even sure what pure and Godly love is. You are not spiritual fruit. You may even find that the following fruit are on your vine, envying, grudging, damaging, deceiving, conniving, slandering, back biting, unforgiving, selfish, spiteful, hurtful, ungrateful and hateful and not trustworthy. Believe me when I say. These are the fruit I've seen on some of the saints in leadership.

Being called by God is not season picking– God is God in season and out. Even in apple picking season not every apple is quite ripened for the harvest. BUT one bad apple doesn't spoil the tree. However, in the case of the spiritual leader, his fruit can spoil the bunch.

Be careful when and what you plant. You don't know what's going to grow, all roots aren't good roots. Some need to be cut away. Therefore, when you are called to ministry means you are ready in His service, when you are called to minister means you are prepared to serve.

See the chosen have no choice-you have the ability to hear God for yourself. first you are born again.... You're re-birthed with a new attitude with gratitude, gratefulness flowing from you; you have a divine encounter with the master.... You understand God's specific work.... You have an internal and external vision for life.... There's no denying how good God is.... You're ready to profess and proclaim His Great name.... you have a mandate because you know that you know that you know who He is!!! And seek to carry out further the scripture *For the perfecting of the saints, for the work of the ministry, for the edifying of the body of Christ: Till we all come in the unity of the faith, and of the knowledge of the Son of God, unto a perfect man, unto the measure of the stature of the fullness of Christ:*

As the remainder of year went on, we now reach Christmas day Sunday December 25, 2016. And on that day, I handed in a letter to the person in charge stating my disappointment in where I felt I was in my journey. Let me share the words that were said to me on that very day: *You know next year is your year Evangelist*! I laughed to myself. Part of me felt bad this was Christmas day. And everyone knows how I'm all about that sacred, holy blessed season and the love, joy and peace that surrounds it! I'm very emotional and it's just ALL ABOUT JESUS – as it is ALL year but this time, once Thanksgiving rolls around, I'm just at another level of inner praise. I also 'turn up' around resurrection Sunday as well. That's just me! The God in me! But the letter had to be given. I thought my Church hurt was done! I sense it in my spirit that there is more to come. Instead of leaving this church, I remained for the sake of my husband.

I don't believe in New Year's resolutions; I just believe in being the best vessel of service that I can be for the glory of God. This means being at my best health, mentally and physically and my best health spiritually. As you can see this fiasco is testing my spiritual health.

Well January 2017, I am still pressing and pushing. You all know what it means to push-pray until something happens. But I have come to the point that I feel that my husband should resign his position BUT guess what you know I never ever came flat out to him and asked him. I needed to let him, do him. He has a respectable, prominent position that he had taken on, and I always supported. The fact is, he accepted the position in a meeting and he then came home and told me. I was never given the opportunity to approve or give any consent, I just accepted, congratulated hugged kissed and supported.

Ok so now I come to service and other programs that take place and I'm living with this silent conviction. It's silent because I have not acted on this. Again, I am simply accepting and dealing. I'm a peacemaker, I'm an easy spirit and It's DAMN hard now to face and stay yet another year and my MAMA ain't here to help lessen the blow. Just to keep it real, my mind said. "Oh Hell no!" If I explode and show the real me, then I will bring shame to my husband

and my Lord. But can you understand the need for my physical and emotional well-being? If I hold this in then I'm not being the best healthy version of myself for the Lord. Something has got to give. I simply just want to say, "YO, M----- F ----, time to quit we need to bounce I have to go from here before I die in here!"

Then I had a reality check of myself. The Devil was talking to me now. I felt myself slipping away in silence. I felt that the Holy Spirit was still living inside me, but the fight was on. I was becoming the victim of a declining spirit. You know this Devil! Cleaver, strategic, tactical and his job is to kill steal and destroy. But he knew he had a hard force to contend with (ME). I was not an easy victim. But he knew that the powers that be and those with the control he could use to break me down. Remember he's good at what he does too!

Oh, my attack was real! Now I'm not gullible but I have to play this part so my husband does what he feels is right for the church and the people of the church and most importantly in his mind God. Much respect to that, I love the fact that he's this kind of individual, but it was costing me my sanity. I wasn't my full sanctified self. I wasn't this saint that is only supposed to get better. How am I when I know better but not doing better? I was sacrificing, improvising, but what I really wanted was to just breakdown. I was suffering a spiritual meltdown. Let me explain better: As long as I sit in the pews along with the pew ministry and sing and scream out hallelujah, then I'm no threat to the devils in human form around me. But as soon as I'm sitting and/or ministering from the pulpit, then

I'm a threat to the kingdoms of this world and this "so-called church." Their purpose is satisfied. I needed my husband to understand and digest this concept on his own. Why spell it out in black and white. We are equally yoked right? But I'm all about the WORD so when *Romans 14:19 says Let us therefore make every effort to do what leads to peace and to mutual edification.* I remain neutral and enhance him. I can deal with suffering in silence because the Will of God in me will sustain me in perfect peace. Maybe not now but my faith assures me soon. I can just hold on to God's Unchanging Hand in the meantime. As the lyrics to the popular gospel song remind me, "Trouble don't last always."

This year January 2017 I decided to make a move to elevate myself. Sometimes you must elevate yourself by eliminating a problem. Now although I was still in Berean Bible Institute & School of Ministry during this time, I decided to enroll in United Chaplains State of New York School for a NYS Chaplains license. By this time, I've been working with great physicians professionally for almost seventeen years. I was always visiting the sick and shut in. I was still president of the Compassionate Ministry Team at the church. This burden was placed on my heart and that's where God led me. One of my church brothers introduced me to this particular program as he was enrolled. I did receive the blessing from my pastor to pursue this. I completed the course of study necessary but it was a long process, By God's grace I graduated that October and my husband supported me all the way.

Of course, yes! I am still here to which almost the end of another year. God still gets the glory. He is the joy for my sorrow and my hope for tomorrow and my greatest aspiration. I still desire him. I was getting it ALL back. Be careful that devil doesn't sneak in and start stripping you and devaluing you. YOU must fight hard. I was even saying in my own little head when LL said: 'LL Kool J is hard as hell battle anybody I don't care who you tell I excel they all fail." Well sorry but true I had my own version that I had to be hard as hell battle any devil, I don't care who they tell, I excel and I will not fail.

Part 3

We are here now at New Year 2018. By God I knew something was wrong, terribly wrong. Because I didn't feel the presence of the Holy Spirit at watch night service. That 2016/2017 I thought it was just me. Something was off in the atmosphere but I heard from many members that experienced the same. To be honest, some haven't been back since then. But again 2017/2018 was even a greater stronghold. OMG! Satan took seat and is owning the place- "hello somebody." My worship was feeling quite terminal. I was now concerned because I had an experience on Father's Day Sunday, 2017. I felt a move of God but I ignored it. I'm just being honest. I ignored him because I was trying to justify myself. It's God who justifies us. It's also God who orders us. I know this. But I heard the voice of Jesus clearly and specifically that Sunday on **Father's Day Sunday.** He said He was going to remove me from the hell I was in. The Lord was not listening to my excuses. This God of second, third and many chances was reminding me of His grace and mercy. I ignored the signs because I knew my husband wasn't ready. Then GOD RESPONDED but who was I speaking to? And who does your convictions come through. I could not believe my disobedience God had given me a lifeline and I stayed on the sinking ship. So now continue to **hurt**.

Like I was saying early 2017/2018 I came hurt so I should have known I would leave hurt. Thought having my grandbabies with me would fill the void, persevere go there and just get it over with come home and celebrate. Well its masked things because my babies are my joys next to Jesus and we had fun as always. But that underline hurt still remains day after day, week after week month after month until you reach another year. And know God is still good.

And now it's the second Sunday in January of 2018 I had to speak with the pastor concerning a small matter that required his attention. He says we need to reconcile and start this thing over! I'm telling you that you cannot make this stuff up!!! Oh miss nice, miss easy going, miss big on forgiving again accepted and agreed to yet meeting again and moving forward. LOL and before I go further my LOL. **Is Lord of Lords**?

Well the first and last meeting took place April 2018. It was the three of us and the conversation went well. The putting off was not going to go on any longer and bygones was going to be bygones. We made our peace for past and present; reconciliation was introduced by all party's forgiveness appeared to be activated verbally and it seemingly went pretty well… BUT as you know I been there done that before! Anyways my husband and I left on a good notion and there was supposed to be a follow up meeting in June as May being church anniversary, he was too busy as I was told. And as I'm reminded when minor prophet *Micah* tells us in *6:8 And what does the Lord require of you? To act justly and to love mercy and to walk humbly with your God.* I wasn't ready to walk this journey again-I felt that you know that Devil he would somewhere somehow show up and interfere because of who I am dealing with. Falsely walked away with what I was told. To wait and hear something in June of 2018. You know the old saying fool me once and shame on you-fool me twice shame on me; now what do they say about the third time, looks like I was led to be made a fool of – and in my mind I knew the deal and Mama ain't raise NO fools – so where's the foolery?

I heard nothing! And I suspected I wouldn't here nothing. *{Pay attention to those confirmations that God gives you}.* But I was approached on the 1st Sunday in July by one of my adversaries who chose to share some of her observations and recommendations which I found extremely disrespectful and un warranted even commenting on my dress. Rest assure the June meeting didn't happen for a reason and I NOW know for sure the rest of year was not going to happen either. I'm aware of infiltrators and perpetrators, and since this is the goliath that kept coming for me, I had my last sling shot and I had to make it count. Thank God for the spirit to transform, correct, and protect. Believe me when I tell you I was not always saved… BUT GOD BE THE GLORY I was reminded of just how saved I am on that blessed Lord's Day of July 2018 or I would be writing this from my jail cell. **The Holy Spirit acts and**

**move's fast within you thank God I was able to keep up-
before I was taken back.** You ever used to watch the
Flintstones and the good angel and the bad would be on
each side of Fred's shoulder telling him what to do? He
needed to make a decision quick. THANK GOD for the
blood that never loses its power!!!! That day Jesus jumped
in me before I can leap. Saved by grace… I left singing the
song "God Kept Me". Yessss! He did. God is better to us
than we are to ourselves... be true! I stayed away the
remainder of month for a good reason and those reasons are
the reasons why I am saved today. Because people trying to
give me a reason to just go there! Not a good place. I tell
you at all – not good for me or anyone on the receiving end.
I can hear Earth, Wind & Fire in my ear singing Reasons.
La la la la la la la la…. WHY after all the reasons why????

**It was a do not come for me moment if I don't come for
you!** People get your glory twisted and don't know your
full story!!! Ohhh But God knew to keep me out of there!

*1 Corinthians 10:13 No **temptation** has overtaken you that
is unusual for **human beings**. But God is faithful, and he
will not allow you to be tempted beyond your strength.
Instead, along with the temptation he will also provide a
way out, so that you may be able to endure it.*

*Psalm 34:17-18 The LORD hears those who cry out, and he
delivers them from all their **distress.**18 The LORD is close to
the brokenhearted, and he delivers those whose spirit has
been **crushed**.*

*John 14:26-27 But the **Helper**, the Holy Spirit, whom the
Father will send in my name, will teach you all things and
remind you of everything that I have told you. 27 I'm leaving*

*you at peace. I'm giving you my own peace. I'm not giving it to you as the **world** gives. So don't let your hearts be troubled, and don't be afraid.*

*2 **Corinthians 12:9-10** But he said to me, "My grace is sufficient for you, for my power is made perfect in weakness." Therefore, I will boast all the more gladly of my **weaknesses**, so that the power of Christ may rest upon me. 10 For the sake of Christ, then, I am content with weaknesses, **insults**, hardships, persecutions, and calamities. For when I am weak, then I am strong.*

Let me point out the 2 words in each scripture bolded for you to see how the enemy attacks. See there's a Devil for every level. The higher you go the bigger the Devil. And when I start to piece together how I have been under attack almost seven years in this place and by the same people repeatedly. See Satan temps us and when he can't temp you particularly-he will use another person with a lesser mind to come after you. **Temptation** is strong and the weak are who he preys on because they are weak **human beings** that are of the flesh. Seeking to cause **distress** in your life to offset the miserable life he lives and those who are at his beckon. They want to **crush** you, ravage you, deflect you, disregard you, deploy you, and deprive you. But it's God who we ultimately have and will always have as our **helper.** His majestic and mighty ways is how He sustains us, He is a way maker, a burden bearer and a promise keeper! Just know that in this **world** God helps those who can't help themselves. Even in your time of **weakness** when others criticize, lie and **insult** you and come at you.

God's got you in His hand that's why we trust, we believe and we remain and keep our faith. Faith is in our future, faith is our tomorrow, faith is what we walk by and faithfulness is what we live by.

As I returned the first Sunday of the following month, I knew it was best that I get the Devil off my chest. And address my adversary. It was not going to be one of those excuse me Jesus moments, because I prayed about it and I was taking the cross with me. I spoke my peace and left knowing that I was not expecting to return. The reality is God had to let me know that I am going to hit you with a reminder since you did not leave - now I will just snatch you out! God spoke for me: I only wanted to hash out what took place a few Sundays prior. I was respectful, calm and poise stating that you did not come from a righteous place. And not for nothing my family and especially my Mama put the attire in 'church attire,' I know how to dress in the presence of the Lord! I don't know what you have against me all these years since I first preached but I assure you, you won't have any further problems or concerns from me, enjoy the pulpit, I love you, we know I am never preaching in here again anyhow, I was never accepted up there. So, let's just co-exist in the kingdom, and keep it moving. I felt this was a set up from the start because of the initial interrogation that took place the first Sunday in July. He sent his concubine because our last discussion I pointed out how I was not going to be subject or ridiculed taking orders from some of the others because of seniority because we are all under God's authority. I made it clear that we are on equal ground and he agreed. I had heard about as well I have seen how this particular person acts like the authoritarian.

To approach me about what I am wearing and then describe what I wore that last few Sundays? I knew it was a go for her again moment, the enemy destroys the leadership and I knew; yet another attack to get me to back up from this thing; at least in this place! Really you able to tell me what I wore consecutively the last few Sundays. (I even had to think what the hell I had on) And I am inappropriately dressed today is what I was told! I am going to kick facts: In my mind I'm thinking keep fucking with me!!!

Saying, Touch not mine anointed, and do my prophets no harm. 1 Chronicles 16:22. It was one of those bye Felicia moments OR as I like to say bye Devil! How they say on the street's deuces! I'm out, I need to bounce!!! Be gone. Seven years of humiliation who on Gods earth would have stood or stand for this. That's why I now rather give my enemies a *chair* to let them sit, since I know they can't *stand* to see me blessed. LOL!!!

P.S. *mind you this person told me two years ago you know it took me over 5 years to be accepted by him. Pleaseeee!*

Ministry Shame

You're probably saying ministry shame? What shame is there in ministry? The answer is - it's the shame one faces while in ministry madness. I failed to mention that part of the April 2018 meeting I had with my pastor was to share the honor of me receiving The **Allen Jamison Ensemble Black Women Rock Awards IV** to be held in September. I got a brief congratulations and it was never spoken of again. Only with certain members were their accolades fully acknowledged. But at end of meeting he was able to say to my husband he didn't need to come with me to meetings… *lol*.

The important thing is that when the ceremony took place, the ones who counted came out to support me and it was a glorious event. The keynote speaker was an amazing Bishop and a sistah in the kingdom. She's the dear Overseer that nominated me. I met this dynamitic powerhouse in April 2017 at a prayer breakfast at my church. We exchanged numbers and she been a roll on with Jesus friend ever since; and saw fit to nominate me for such a prestige event after hearing me preach in October 2017 as well.

*1 **Peter 4:16** But if you suffer as a Christian, do not be ashamed, but glorify God that you bear that name.*

I want to go back to the original shame placed on me. Back on Sunday January 25, 2015. It was Sunday morning 10:30 service I was speaker/preacher for the Compassionate Ministry Anniversary (I do thank those that really campaigned for me to get that platform as I know it wasn't easy).

The shame came into play when on the Wednesday before, while I went over my sermon with the Pastor. I was told I could not preach from the pulpit but from the podium because I was not Clergy and it was sacred. It was both interesting and ironic that my adversary was the only other person that knew I was told that. LOL… So, I said fine, sure I understand its 'holy ground'.

I was honestly a touch displaced however was so excited about the word that I had to give to God's people I tried to get past it. But insult was added to injury when his lackey had the nerve to approach me that Sunday morning and say "you know you can't go up in the pulpit and don't greet the people" when everyone saw the church filled to capacity with guests that were there in support of me and the Compassion Ministry. Well when I look back to that moment, I know I was under God's protection. Why the need to drive the stake further in my heart and to do it right before I was to give a word from God. What was the point, what was your motivation?

For a leader to put shame on you in front of everybody, the entire congregation and guests. But it's as if they have no shame about their own actions. They preach from this pulpit and stand before God's people a Holy Representative yet treat me so differently. How interesting that I am the very person that clearly told you that I did not care about any of the negative things that I am aware of regarding you, I'm just trying to preach God's word and win souls. You even claimed to have appreciate that since much of it can't be disputed. I never talked about it or disclosed it; that's not what drives me.

I was left feeling stripped and rapped spiritually and you still stand before God and the people from that very same pulpit that you found humor with the smirk on your face telling me I couldn't stand and preach from it. The kicker of what happened that day was the outpouring and overjoyed support from my friends, loved ones, and supporters on that magnificent Sunday.

Mama was there with tears in her eyes as it was almost a year since she had been diagnosed with congestive heart failure and renal failure at 92 Lord's year's age.

Now people of God! I respect the pulpit just as much as the next Christian. Sacred and holy it is. {What I really wanted to say then why are you? And some of them preaching from it}? I mean come on with these theatrics. But I'm respectable to authority but that was true. I didn't say but its facts! BECAUSE ONE THING I MUST SHARE WITH THE WORLD IS SOMETHING SO HOLY AND SACRED THEN HOW IS THAT ANYBODY, I MEAN ANYBODY SHOULD REALLY STAND AND PREACH FROM IT AS WHO ON EARTH DESERVES TOO? (*Get the idea I mean it should be absent ground for anybody to stand on*)

Quite frankly, souls aren't being saved, minds aren't being transformed and hearts aren't being delivered. Let me further say you do know that the pulpit is just sacred and blessed furniture and Jesus never preached from it! Anyone who stands in a pulpit really stand before God and the people with expectancy to be invited back again-so what did that leave me to expect? Come on I'm talking right! But I knew the real deal – ok, got it, let's keep it moving. Demons up in here putting demands on things. I wasn't concerned about that!!! I was focused on the Word for the people something some of them in there are still missing, not getting, not hearing, not receiving, not comprehending, not understanding, and it's a problem.

Jeremiah 7:8 But look, you are trusting in deceptive words that are worthless.

But yet God prevails and that blessed glorious Sunday morning Great is thy faithfulness… Well if you thought the hater hated you before it shows now, they just can't stand you! Moments like that you say let your haters be your helpers and the takers get taken while the fakers just need to face it! They not going to stop until you die! Then want to sing and shout at your funeral like they oh so hurt but the hearts of them want to kick dirt on your grave. Don't they know HELL is rejoicing now over their behavior? You keep giving him an entrance to come in, come by and reside. Not me, I want to reside under the shadow of the almighty. I'm not about to be indoctrinated into the Devils kingdom! I want the doctrine of the Holy Spirit! They continue to act up. They don't ascertain nor have acquired the knowledge that the book of ACTS means not to perform in a theater. They think it means come to church to act up not come to the house to worship. How can you claim to walk with God, yet holding the Devils hand, and stepping on Gods people Sunday after Sunday? But their definition of church biblical history means their way or no way.

A - I am a Believer

Galatians 2:20 *I am crucified with Christ: nevertheless I live; yet not I, but Christ liveth in me: and the life which I now live in the flesh I live by the faith of the Son of God, who loved me, and gave himself for me.*

That's what I believed, and lived by. I was alive in Christ!

Remember Colin Kaepernick had to do something because not of just believing, but it was his conviction that caused him to take a knee. God bless that brother. Sometimes people watch you, they study you, they think they know you, and some draw they own perception of you. While some like you and others hate you! Well they knew he was a good football player but underestimated his perception. Of what he felt was right, his definition of what he had believed. What was at stake here is WHAT WOULD IT COST HIM?

I myself truly understand. That he believed in something even if it means sacrificing everything. Well I believe in God enough that I would do anything that the Holy Spirit compels and tells me to do! As I had to walk away from twelve years of service at a church that killed my spirits. (Jesus has left the building) figuratively and literally. It killed me to leave, but I was dead if I stayed. The devil wearing me out, taking me out and trying to cancel me out. I mean I was losing every round with the devil!!!

As Colin Kaepernick had enough-I had enough of this demon beating.

It was I Pledge Allegiance to the Flag of the United States of America, and to the Republic for which it stands, one Nation under God, indivisible, with Liberty and Justice for all.

For me it was I Plead the blood for which it stands, To the World Jesus saves, One nation under God, The Father, Son and the Holy Spirit, invisible, with Liberty, Justice, Salvation and Peace for all.

B - I Trust in Him

See God sent Archangel Michael to be an angel of WARFARE that conquers Satan. As we know from *Daniel 12:1 At that time Michael, the great prince who protects your people, will arise. There will be a time of distress such as has not happened from the beginning of nations until then. But at that time your people—everyone whose name is found written in the book—will be delivered.* Michael commands God's army against Satan's forces as told in the Book of *Revelation 12:7-9 Then war broke out in heaven. Michael and his angels fought against the dragon, and the dragon and his angels fought back. 8 But he was not strong enough, and they lost their place in heaven. 9 The great dragon was hurled down—that ancient serpent called the devil, or Satan, who leads the whole world astray. He was hurled to the earth, and his angels with him.*

As God had sent Gabriel to be His WORD angel that went to Zechariah in **Luke 1:19** *The angel answered him, "I'm Gabriel! I stand in God's presence. God sent me to tell you this good news.* That same WORD angel visited Mary in **Luke 28** *When the angel entered her home, he greeted her and said, "You are favored by the Lord! The Lord is with you."*

When you know God has fired Lucifer and that He's still on the throne looking for WORSHIPPERS, us/we, His people then you need to know that there's work to be done to be fulfilled and carried out! Allow God to move you to the next level a new dimension. There's a practice of praise in affect that God is calling mankind, that the God of Divinity is seeking humanity to carry out His work and His will.

Never mind the blood suckers, venomous, toxic, negative people, remember Maya Angelou tells us, *"When people show you who they are, believe them."* So, know that you even got to push back on those who **PREY** on you, they are anti you, against you, not for you, they feel you are a threat. They don't like you, don't want to receive you-so they *prey* on you. They succumb to their level of insecurity. But you have to know *that with God be for you, WHO can be against you?* I believe that ALL things are possible with God but everything and anything is impossible without Him.

The closer you get with the one who is your problem solver, you begin to pay the problem makers no attention. They are a pact of noisemakers and hell raisers thinking that their titles and positions will get them into heaven no matter how much hell they keep raising. You blowing up in the Holy Spirit and they're trying to blow you away. You begin singing like McFadden and Whitehead *'Aint no Stopping us/ME Now-we on the Move.'*

C - My Spirit Affected

You are in the fight of your life; this is World War Us. This is also a Christian War because. There are too many saying the name of Jesus but they are still in their personal body of selfishness, lust, greed, gluttony, idolatry and flesh. To add insult to injury These are the worst spirits to possess. Because they are never satisfied. Those are the spirits at the core of their being and ultimately their decision making. They are vengeful in their own victory. A murderer and a rapist will feel less remorse than those that have a spirit of Lust, greed and idolatry. Paul will confirm just read your bible.

I had to let God change my perspective. I put people on a pedestal giving them too much credit because of degrees and titles. Maybe I get thirsty myself to tell the truth. I admitted before wanting something badly because I thought I belonged. Well it took me sometime to realize I only belong to Him. He shielded my dark days, protected my weary nights and it was God keeping me from that Devil's den. OH Thank you Jesus! Won't He do it?!!! Taught me to Let go, let it flow and go… I bet God Himself thought I was crazy.

See, I just love Paul. I even told a leader once who asked me who I relate myself to in the bible. I SAID PAUL. This is true, I wrote a letter and all explaining it. Because of the road to Damascus was such a perfect experience and I didn't put any of that in my letter, but I just wanted to share and point out CHANGE: which we are called to as born again Christians. Paul is the teacher of change. As well he teaches us to be servants and good stewards and that everything is ALL about God.

2 Corinthians 2:17 For we are not as many, which corrupt the word of God: but as of sincerity, but as of God, in the sight of God speak we in Christ.

2 Corinthians 4:2 Rather, we have renounced secret and shameful ways; we do not use deception, nor do we distort the word of God. On the contrary, by setting forth the truth plainly we commend ourselves to everyone's conscience in the sight of God.

Paul speaks of the false preachers who undermine ministry. Peter talks of it, others speak on it and WOW listen to how Jeremiah with that word WOE;

Jeremiah 23:1-4 Woe be unto the pastors that destroy and scatter the sheep of my pasture! saith the LORD.
2 Therefore thus saith the LORD God of Israel against the pastors that feed my people; Ye have scattered my flock, and driven them away, and have not visited them: behold, I will visit upon you the evil of your doings, saith the LORD.

3 And I will gather the remnant of my flock out of all countries whither I have driven them, and will bring them again to their folds; and they shall be fruitful and increase.

4 And I will set up shepherds over them which shall feed them: and they shall fear no more, nor be dismayed, neither shall they be lacking, saith the LORD.

That scripture gave me happiness, comfort, satisfaction, joy, peace, assurance and knowing in the midst of my suffering, hurt and spiritual attack that I was good!!! I was just done after that scripture. Because I know more than loving Christ and loving my family, I wanted to be under a leader to pour into and continuously edify, exhort, counsel, train and Shepherd me and help me to walk this Christian journey I was on a mission!!!

D - A Life with Christ

I only have this one thing to say, that I always say I love to say I will continue to say and many of you heard me say it time and time again: ***"God sent Jesus to inaugurate His kingdom on earth; a life without Christ is missing out on the best part of living."***

Christ is my life! For me, my family and everything attached, surrounding and/or a part of me. In ALL THINGS-which means any and everything I do, everywhere I go, and in any place and every breath that I take He is with me. Let everything that has breathe praise ye the Lord! No matter what you are going through or dealing with - *In the good and the bad, the happy or sad, the bitter or sweet, the evil and nice, the pretty and the ugly, the joy and the sorrow, the truth and the lies, the kind or the mean, the ups the downs, the highs and lows, the wrongs the rights, the tempted and the loyal, the distrust and the trusted, the tried and true, the wicked and the righteous, the fails and the flourish, the sick and the salvation, the gloom and the glory, the pain and the passion, the burden and the blessings the hooray and the hurt.* ALL THINGS!!! God goes with me and is in me. My walk, my talk. He is my ALL and ALL!!! Understand when **Romans 8:28** *And we know that all things work together for good to them that love God, to them who are the called according to his purpose.* It does not matter what you've been through, what you're going through its ALL things understand that concept of knowledge.

Even back in **Genesis** it was told to Abraham *God is with 'you'/us in everything we do.*

That's why I love to greet people with 'Abundant Blessings!' *{Most say grace and peace or bless you, or my brother or sister, some say praise the Lord}* I just like greeting people with '**abundant blessings**' because spiritual abundance is life. That not only in ALL things is He but He is above ALL things and He's above ALL!!!

Ephesians 3:20 *Now unto him that is able to do exceedingly abundantly above all that we ask or think, according to the power that worketh in us,*

The word abundance/abundant/abundantly is frequently mentioned in the Bible as something God offers to those who trust in Him. It's our belief of just how big God is! God will provide an abundant life to those who "seek first the kingdom of God and His righteousness." Abundance means a life full of everything you need to sustain yourself in joy, peace and purpose. If we first give God our life, He **will** bless us in ways that we can never imagine; we live in abundance. God gave His son first to us. So, life more abundantly translates to a life in and with Christ! Not a piece not a portion but our whole life our entire life, not part time – ALL the time.

2 Corinthians 9:8 And God is able to bless you abundantly, so that in all things at all times, having all that you need, you will abound in every good work.

Even in our closing and you sealing the benediction that means we are in agreement with one another, in unison, together we agree in one body in Christ. It's a unified acceptance on who we trust and confirms what we believe. That in Jude exceeding is great, it's abundance.

Jude 24-25 Now unto him that is able to keep you from falling, and to present you faultless before the presence of his glory with exceeding joy,

25 To the only wise God our Saviour, be glory and majesty, dominion and power, both now and ever. Amen. This seals our deal.

WHY MY HUSBAND STAYED

GENESIS 28:15 *I am with you and will watch over you wherever you go, and I will bring you back to this land. I will not leave you until I have done what I have promised you.*

God will not leave you until His promise is fulfilled. That's my husband demeanor, his outlook and his perspective. He holds a position in the church that he takes great pride in, and no different than on his job for the last twenty-seven years. It's important to him. He feels that what he does and what he's doing for the church is for the people of the church. He loves the seniors, the children, the saints and the people that don't have a voice-but he also wants the people to see he carries out his promises to them. My husband is a true man of valor. He is Respected, decent, honorable, genuine, sincere, caring, compassionate, kind and loving. There is an old saying, *"how you get him is how you keep him"*, or *"if a man's not going your way-then he just in your way."*. There is another saying that says, "he was too good for me and too good to be true." …. Well these are his qualities and attributes. He was raised right and truly had a good upbringing. Really, I'm not just saying this. There's so much I can say about the TWENTY years knowing this particular man that I love and chose me as his wife fourteen years ago.

His dedication was in action. My husband was serving his fourth year as the Chairman of the trustee board. He made a lot of people happy, pleased, and proud.

1 Corinthians 12:18 - *But now hath God set the members every one of them in the body, as it hath pleased him.*

Proverbs 16:3 - *Commit thy works unto the LORD, and thy thoughts shall be established.*

My husband has a pure heart. I never worried or distrusted anything since I met him. Truth is I thought he was too good for me and deserved better than me. But he stated, I'm my own worst enemy in this relationship by prejudging. Keep in mind, YES, I was saved when I met him. But saved with a past, I came to the table with far less to offer other than being faithful and love him. And that's what he wanted besides his love for nails that strike me as odd until time went on. But it was simply just a passion he has. There can be other things that he was (and he wasn't) and that may not have been good. And I can say he was one good man for sure. Brought up and lived right. And I was blessed in life to meet him and go on to live out our godly life together as man and wife.

Our joining the church together resurrection 2006 as I previously mentioned after we were married the year before. This was to hopefully fulfill that desire of mine. Anyhow things changed and he was asked to join the trustee board and then he was given the position of chairman. I have to admit that while I was not completely happy, I accepted and congratulated and was HAPPY for him [understand the difference] There were other unfulfilled things taking place. I'm so neutral, so considerate of others over and above myself. He was a prestige type-if he can do something better, he would do it! So, this was where he dove in head first and I was still standing at the shore line.

Galatians 5:22 But the fruit of the Spirit is love, joy, peace, patience, kindness, goodness, faithfulness

I know his integrity and dignity means a lot. Getting the job done and others satisfied in the process was his desire. He doesn't like to upset or anger people or be disloyal to anyone. This was his natural being and he loved and FEARED the Lord truly!!!

Everyone knew how close we are. Ride or die we understood that our marriage was not ME and HIM But it was God and us! We were about our Father's business. NOW here I told my husband he was the Barak of the church as Obama was to the country.

Seriously things were not good and the financial books were in the red and he did everything he could to get them into the black. Projects started getting done and all that! OK good. But he wasn't ready to leave because he had other obligations and responsibilities to fulfill.

My question was, what about responsibilities and obligations to me? *{I was NOT RIGHT}* because the same reasons that kept me there as long as I did/we did in the past are the same reasons and things he deemed necessary to stay now and finish and carry out. He lives on commitment and seeing things through. Committed to us YES but this was a different dynamic and I had to seek God out the more for further understanding because aren't we equally yoked? Yes, we are indeed. So, I thank God for working on me, even though I was hurting inside, not knowing how to handle this and is he putting the church before me? This is a different level of "husbands love your wives as Christ love the church."

Ephesians 5:22-26 Wives, submit yourselves to your own husbands as you do to the Lord. 23 For the husband is the head of the wife as Christ is the head of the church, his body, of which he is the Savior. 24 Now as the church submits to Christ, so also wives should submit to their husbands in everything. 25 Husbands, love your wives, just as Christ loved the church and gave himself up for her

I know my husband loves me unconditionally but hey you see my pain you see my frustrations. I'm dying here. I am devastated and destroyed from that place; you see my cries you know what it's done! BUT when you hear from God, He will reveal to you what He says to you and you need to hear him. The Lord said to me, **"My child your convictions are not on anybody else but you! Your convictions are not his convictions."**

We both knew that we weren't going to be in two different places, but yet I was the one waiting on him. Here I am Lord it's me again. Praying and watching and watching and yet praying. Because this now began to be very stressful and taking a toll on me/us to some degree. In a word we were separated in the house of God. Oh, this has got to be temporary. Something has got to give fast! I'm about to lose my mind in this distress. He's buried in projects and church functions. Talk about a spiritual HEART ATTACK, and although they didn't scandalize my name-they scandalized my spirit, paralyzed my spirit, hemmed my spirit up, real church hurt!

Now here's where it gets good. My husband loves poetry. In the past we would go to poetry spots in the village which inspired him. He now started writing his own spoken word-and for the first time he did this on the men's day service in October 2018. Then again, he did it for the pastor's appreciation service in November and then on December 31 in the watch night service and the fourth time being in January for the

MLK program. Yes, he was approved to do the Spoken Word the last four months consecutively; and I was not allowed to preach there in the last four years. If that was not a spiritual attack then what the hell was it?

I was bruised and torn between the rejection of what seems as preferential treatment for my husband over me by my church and the celebration of his success.

See God will reveal things to you that others will not see {as they are not supposed to} but God reveals to you specifically to show you the trick of the enemy. The cleverness, how strategic and tactful your enemies are. They play mind manipulation games to prove their unrighteous point of lies and deceit. But I tell the world this *until the day they wake up before Christ that's the only way they're going to fool me! And I don't see nobody waking up before Christ!* So, I will participate in this game of checkers because it is not chess. I am a wise woman and I don't have to prove my Godly wisdom to anyone. THANK GOD for the gift. *2 Corinthians 9:15 Thanks be to God for his inexpressible gift!* A wise woman no man can fool no matter what His title.

You even need to keep your faith even in the foolishness. Part of my being saved is knowing the gift God instilled within me. When I wasn't sure I tapped into the Holy Spirit *James 1:5 If any of you lacks wisdom, let him ask God, who gives generously to all without reproach, and it will be given him.* I was very much aware of what was taking place-and I was clear about what was being done. Falsifying God's people that did not know better or any different. Justifying the WOE, it's me. BUT don't you know you can't pretend with God?!!!

His gift His discernment, His revelation is ALL real. It comes together in the certainty that when you know, that you know, that you know.

1 Corinthians 12:7-11 To each is given the manifestation of the Spirit for the common good. For to one is given through the Spirit the utterance of wisdom, and to another the utterance of knowledge according to the same Spirit, to another faith by the same Spirit, to another gifts of healing by the one Spirit, to another the working of miracles, to another prophecy, to another the ability to distinguish between spirits, to another various kinds of tongues, to another the interpretation of tongues. All these are empowered by one and the same Spirit, who apportions to each one individually as he wills.

My husband was blessed with another gift! Not only in his assertion in the board of trustees, but God gave him new revelation. He is able to give a Spoken Word in ministry. He is wonderful at it! The exhortation deliverance and it's well written. He was very well received all four times. Yes, I am his biggest cheerleader and supporter. God equipped him in Spoken Word ministry and he is also a gifted creative writer in the secular world. I loved his ambition, tenacity and how poised he was from the very first time. God used him mightily in his newly acquired gift.

Romans 12:6 Having gifts that differ according to the grace given to us, let us use them: if prophecy, in proportion to our faith;

But I was disappointed in the plot and plan behind the enemies' doors. My husband wouldn't want to believe it! BUT trust me I knew the real deal; because the devil you know is better than the devil you don't. I saw and knew that if some can have it their way; would have loved to see us broken up, separated and apart... Just waiting and anticipating on it!

James 1:17 Every good gift and every perfect gift is from above, coming down from the Father of lights with whom there is no variation or shadow due to change.

1 Peter 4:10 As each has received a gift, use it to serve one another, as good stewards of God's varied grace:

You know my husband also involved himself in so many variations of other things in and around the church that he just did out of the goodness and kindness of his heart. I don't mean to say it lightly- I mean a lot, that's a whole other story. But used at times, yes but he wanted to as he allowed it because he never viewed or looked at it as such but viewed as what he did for the church and the people of the church as helping.

1 Corinthians 14:12 So with yourselves, since you are eager for manifestations of the Spirit, strive to excel in building up the church. 1 John 4:16 So we have come to know and to believe the love that God has for us. God is love, and whoever abides in love abides in God, and God abides in him

The answer to my husband staying a while longer is dedication, trust, faith, hope and his love for the church and its people. My response/assignment was to just simply hold on to God's unchanging hand and just continue to hold on. Trouble don't/won't last always.

Romans 12:3-8 For by the grace given to me I say to everyone among you not to think of himself more highly than he ought to think, but to think with sober judgment, each according to the measure of faith that God has assigned. For as in one body we have many members, and the members do not all have the same function, so we, though many, are one body in Christ, and individually members one of another. Having gifts that differ according to the grace given to us, let us use them: if prophecy, in proportion to our faith; if service, in our serving; the one who teaches, in his teaching;

I do know this: He might not approve everything we ask for. But if your prayers align with His purpose for your life, then you can be confident that they will come to pass. As I knew this too shall eventually pass.

And to sum it up I knew my husband was walking in authority. That's the only way to walk.

Psalms 37:23 - The steps of a [good] man are ordered by the LORD: and he delighteth in his way.

HEALING FROM THE HURT

Psalm 123 Unto thee lift I up mine eyes, O thou that dwellest in the heavens. 2 Behold, as the eyes of servants look unto the hand of their masters, and as the eyes of a maiden unto the hand of her mistress; so our eyes wait upon the LORD our God, until that he have mercy upon us. 3 Have mercy upon us, O LORD, have mercy upon us: for we are exceedingly filled with contempt. 4 Our soul is exceedingly filled with the scorning of those that are at ease, and with the contempt of the proud.

Me in contempt, that's how I felt, that's what I received, that's how I was treated, that's what they wanted me to believe. When you are spiritually deprived and raped, your spiritual man feels suffocated. You better fight back with the divine power of the holy spirit and fast and pray and know that it's time to slay some giants, destroy some Devils, and destroy some demons, and kick Satan's ass! You are slumming, crying, balling and wailing like you don't know the Master, the maker and creator, the alpha and omega, the beginning and the end! AND

CHECK this out: it ain't over until God say's it's over. *Pick yourself up, dust off the mess, shake that crazy off you, and get back on the kingdom train-ride in glory, you been flying high and your plain hasn't crashed, what you stopping for? I'm singing that ole song 'What has been joined by God, let no man put asunder'.* I think God even asked me "what the hell wrong with me." I know good and well better!" I know my Mama certainly was going upside my head GET THIS FOOLISHNESS OUT OF YOU NOW!!! You know you must have faith even in the midst of the foolishness and the foolery.

Psalm 124 If it had not been the LORD who was on our side, now may Israel say;

2 If it had not been the LORD who was on our side, when men rose up against us:

3 Then they had swallowed us up quick, when their wrath was kindled against us:

4 Then the waters had overwhelmed us, the stream had gone over our soul:

5 Then the proud waters had gone over our soul.

6 Blessed be the LORD, who hath not given us as a prey to their teeth.

7 Our soul is escaped as a bird out of the snare of the fowlers: the snare is broken, and we are escaped.

8 Our help is in the name of the LORD, who made heaven and earth.

The Psalms was looking and sounding good. And when I thought about lift up your head - - -.

Psalm 24:7-10 *Lift up your heads, O ye gates; and be ye lift up, ye everlasting doors; and the King of glory shall come in.*
8 Who is this King of glory? The LORD strong and mighty, the LORD mighty in battle.

9 Lift up your heads, O ye gates; even lift them up, ye everlasting doors; and the King of glory shall come in.

10 Who is this King of glory? The LORD of hosts, he is the King of glory. Selah.

I began shouting. I was buried and swallowed I mean looking down all doom and gloom literally physically, emotionally, mentally, spiritually. I know I am certified Christ, I breath Jesus, I am pro and ALL everything Jesus, I am joined with Christ, I am united in Christ, I live life loving Christ everybody hears me say it, I sign papers and end letters stating that! The song goes 'Forever is a long time that's how long I'll love you forever' AND here you act like you losing your way. Well that's how I felt! Watch out for that spirit of deception, manipulation and confusion that will alter your inner spirits, that spirit that comes to rob you and strip you from everything you believe. It's a spirit of *h*arm, *u*nfulfilled, *r*otten, *t*rouble-that spells HURT!

I do know that manipulation can never overtake manifestation. The way things start out is not the way they end up. Twelve years ago, up until now I fully understand that when God is involved-His movement trumps everything! That means things I wanted, things I expected, things I thought, things I intended to happen, things I thought I needed, things I desired; well His purpose may not be what you say but it's always what God says. His way and His will. He holds and He has your/our destiny in his hands. That even when you're faced with humiliation you have to know that grace still applies. And while it looks like one thing, God is doing another thing. I spoke to myself that I can't rebuke people that refuse God's Word! And I cannot sit here and regret being the good person to the wrong people. Self-help: hurts then it heals.

'Seek his truth' worship Him in spirit and in truth. In true worship you hear God, for all those around you hollering and not listening are ONLY hearing themselves-hearing nothing from God and nothing from nothing leaves nothing. And with the noise they just breeding Satan's territory. We shouldn't shun and overlook disregard our co-laborers or put them out the pasture with malicious antics and deprive them and suppress their gifts. Where is multi ministry in that? Where is the ministry amongst the saints in that? By allowing any other spirit to overtake you like that of envy or jealousy that we can't or won't embrace others gifts and talents. A diversity in our gifts leads to diversity in ministry. Bridging, building, expanding, exceling, enlarging, broadening God's heavenly and divine Kingdom. We begin to manifest His power, His glory. When we honor God and love others, we help advance the Kingdom. We want to materialize, multiply, maximize and magnify the Kingdom of God-*not* deflate, infiltrate, neglect and minimize.

Psalm 34:1-3 I will bless the LORD at all times: his praise shall continually be in my mouth.
2 My soul shall make her boast in the LORD: the humble shall hear thereof, and be glad.

3 O magnify the LORD with me, and let us exalt his name together.

I spent over twelve years and seven of them I felt like I was immobilized in my spirit. My Spirit was hijacked. You know the more you try to come up **the more Devils show up.** This was one of the most despicable and disreputable things to happen to someone in the house of the Lord.

As stated before, the church of God is where we should be allowed to worship freely from Sunday to Sunday without fear of the carnality from the world to seep in. Thank God that through all this, the Holy Spirit led me to find an exit strategy for me to seek refuge. Our God is extraordinary.

Revelation 21:5 He who was seated on the throne said, "I am making everything new!" Then he said, "Write this down, for these words are trustworthy and true."

I told you about trust and to believe. God is much more than we can actually ever see or will ever comprehend. Let's start with first things first! GOD IS LOVE! LOVE IS GOD!!! Again, *For God so loved the world* you know the rest!

This God! That raised Jesus from the dead, that made the blind to see, the lame to walk, the deaf to hear, who fed 5000 with five loaves of bread and two fish, the one who is the bread of life, the one who turned water into wine. He's the God who a woman with a blood disease twelve years touched and was made whole. He's the same God who spoke to the woman at the well to change.

He's the God of Abraham, Isaac and Jacob, the God who delivered Ruth, the God who showed favor to Moses, the God that anointed David, the God that walked on water and the God who parted the red seas, the God who raised Lazarus from the dead, the God who answered Elijah, a God that will remember you, and fight for you, and prosper you, and protect you. He is a God who will deliver you, and use you, keep you, the God that does ALL these things and more. I can go through the bible of OUR GOD! The miracle worker! My God that transformed Paul on that Damascus road. I can give scripture after scripture. And I will never understand how we are not interpreting and acquiring and understanding and gaining God's knowledge and ability. Even if you read the bible *backwards* you will still get the same goodness because your revelation of Him started from the beginning to the end

NO WEAPON FORMED against you will prosper. This statement encapsulates my experiences so far. The enemy can plan but he will never succeed.

Now people can give commentary after every scripture, right? But let me ask-who's talking or commenting on bad church behavior such as the saints acting up certainly not understanding the book of ACTS! Nor any of the other 65 books in the bible. Or anything that the church is designed to do. How can you grow and build if you're tearing people down?

You have to look to the hills from which comes your help in time of spiritual trouble! My help cometh from the Lord…. You should know that the devil wears high heels, pretty dresses and custom-tailored suits too. In fact, the devil shops where you shop and wears exactly what you wear as well. The devil doesn't show up in long horns and a cape, the fact is he or she doesn't have an actual mugshot. The devil looks like whoever is available for his bidding. The enemy had me in **ministry misery!** I know I may not be perfect I have faults and failures but I guarantee this and I'll give you 100 witnesses to agree this is me:

Psalm 139:23-24 Search me, O God, and know my heart: try me, and know my thoughts: 24 And see if there be any wicked way in me, and lead me in the way everlasting.

CONFESSION

I would like to say this: just like when you're sick or badly ill you go to the doctor or hospital ER because you know you need to get well. Or at least hoping and praying as you put your trust in the doctor or physician.

When you coming to the church for spiritual healing and you continuously find that you are not, then seek some professional help. Get spiritual counsel, see a therapist, a Bishop, a Pastor, a Priest or a Rabbi. Be sure they have impeccable credentials in that area to help you because people come to the church for help and if they're being hurt, then there's a problem.

That's why we are losing to the outside world! They are looking at us as the biggest hypocrites. Let me share that you can spiral out of control, lose your mind and have thoughts of suicide. *I once said Lord if I can't preach your Word to the people than what am I living for?* Yes!!! It's real thoughts real dealings in real life, and because of the hurt, people have taken their life. Not everybody can deal with rejection or termination from something [ie: job] being once rich-wealthy and lost it all; or just life's ups and downs, they start binge drinking alcohol, turn to drugs while slipping away in sorrow. * **So, they take what they think is an escape.** That's why I know suicide, depression, oppression is real! Sinner, saint or Christian you need to know just how real it is. Consider *Your sanity vs. being saved.* So, I may not get how people in corporate, politics, or Christianity react to that. BUT I will say I understand the world dishes out and delivers a high level of hurt and pain that it's NOT completely easy for everybody to PUSH their way through.

I became a spiritual wimp! I was spiritually wasted, spiritually, wounded, spiritually worn out to sum it up: at my **spiritual worst.**

That real dark place. It's a silent and weak killer. Preying and exercising with our everyday life and thoughts. It's an excruciating feeling on the mind. It's strong, it's controlling, and mind blowing. It will have you wake up with a new mind and it's not a mind stayed on Christ! It's something unexplainable but real and possible. That you end it all, and then it's too late that some people never get to witness how darkness can turn to marvelous light. Get help for your distraught and distressed moments. It's essential before it becomes critical.

BACK TO HEALING FROM THE HURT

L et's face it, there's a ministry attraction some folks possess, they want it for the fame, fortune or the glamour and some have in their minds that oh I'm definitely going to heaven if I am in ministry - God won't send me to hell. All of these are not the right reasons but, we feel are true.

There's a price to obtain a position in ministry. Jesus paid it ALL – ALL to Him I owe! I sought it and chased it because I just love people once I became saved. My love is a part of helping and caring. I am fascinated with the WORD of the Lord. I am elated and I marvel at the scriptures. That when I read them it does something to me… motivates and I say people can really change, the world can change, the world could be better, the world could do better. I just acquired and continue to just have this desire to care for people. We can all be human motivators to one another. Scriptures move you and compel you as you are being delivered and transformed and saved. It's the re-birthing process that we go through and experience. Praise be to God for His inspirations that inspires me and has kept me. One of my favorite scriptures is:

*2 **Timothy 3:16** All scripture is given by inspiration of God, and is profitable for doctrine, for reproof, for correction, for instruction in righteousness:*

There's meaning in the WORD. The Word is for us! It is words to live by. I thank God that I was able to survive the ministry madness after being blackballed and railroaded and faced with opposition and resentment I was topsy-turvy. BUT God He is just who He says He is. Good for me good for us! God is the rock of our salvation. I just want to see a world paradigm shift, world change, world peace. If you are going through your season of betrayal denial or rejection, don't doubt the hand of God.

That's all happening for a reason of more preparation for the position. It's not a death sentence. It's not the end of the world. You have faith, you have His grace and His mercy, and you have trust to believe on the everlasting savior. The master hears all he knows all and he's in ALL because He is ALL. If my Mama was here, she'd be singing one of her favorite hymns *'My Hope is Built on Nothing less than Jesus blood and Righteousness I dare not trust the sweetest frame but wholly lean on Jesus name. On Christ the solid rock I stand ALL other ground is sinking sand!'*

I felt blatantly disrespected as a human and disregarded as a parishioner. But what was part of the straw that broke the camel's back, or the icing on the cake is when someone thinks it's OK to publicly negate you as clergy in the presence of others on purpose to further humiliate and shame you even after you received license and a title. *But like I said those titles are not power to slander and damage and be rude because you have some authority.* I don't really care that you don't want to acknowledge my position that's OK but you are not going to make it obvious in my face and in front of the entire congregation. I was treated like I was some prisoner in the church. Understand, I was not about to sit under someone, or anyone that I don't understand how they think it's OK to do what they do - but when you figure it out, knowing that God is not in their equation – remove yourself.

Example: When I was asked to read scripture at a funeral, every minister reads it from the pulpit-I was directed to the podium. Even *while the other minister who sits on the pulpit of course read from up there.* Is that not outright humiliation? Even after I became a minister. You can't make this up!

When asked to do the church anniversary altar call; that's done every Sunday from the pulpit by those that have titles, even from some who have no title *(let's keep that real)*-I was directed to the podium.

Same on any other ministry anniversaries-I received signal to approach the podium. Other members saw it and expressed concern and even offered apologies. I appreciated them, and there was no need as I was good.

Let's face it, if I wasn't going to be hurt in there-I certainly wasn't going to be healed in there. My showing up was like pulling on a door that says push.... or pushing on a door that says pull.

I'm not this perfect saint-I have never claimed to be. I have problems, issues, flaws and faults like anybody else. There were times when there were some good things that happened and took place for me there-I truly thank God for it. The reality is the bad outweighed and superseded the good. After all, twelve years had to be something right? But I have no regrets because life is a learning lesson, life is opportunity, life is challenging, life is a struggle, life is even an adventure, life is not easy.

Ephesians 6:11-18 *King James Version (KJV)*
11 Put on the whole armour of God, that ye may be able to stand against the wiles/schemes of the devil.
12 For we wrestle/struggle not against flesh and blood, but against principalities, against powers, against the rulers/authorities of the darkness of this world, against spiritual forces/wickedness in high places.
13 Wherefore take unto you the whole/full armour of God, that ye may be able to withstand in the evil day, and having done all, to stand.
14 Stand therefore firm, having your loins girt about with truth/belt of truth buckled, and having on the breastplate of righteousness;
15 And your feet shod with the preparation/readiness of the gospel of peace;
16 Above all, taking the shield of faith, wherewith ye shall be able to quench/extinguish all the fiery darts/flaming arrows of the wicked/evil.
17 And take the helmet of salvation, and the sword of the Spirit, which is the word of God:
18 Praying all occasions/always with all prayer and supplication in the Spirit, with this in mind/and watching

thereunto with all perseverance/be alert and supplication for all saints; the Lord's people.

This is how one remains; remember we must rely on trusting God. The reproof, reproach, reciprocity, repeal, reprimand, repetition, resolution, and revelation ALL come from God; that's our greatest inspiration and our greatest reward, that's how he becomes our refugee, our only resource. Even when a spiritual assault comes on or you become spiritually wounded you must learn and discern how to listen for God's spiritual intellect.

His Intel, His instructions. If you don't it will further silence you in ministry misery. And you need spiritual insight-God's vision. The enemy will have your vision obscured, astigmatism, even tunnel vision, blinding you scales and coal so thick you can't see straight or even think right. Taking your mind completely from *Let this mind be in you, which was also in Christ Jesus: Who, being in the form of God, thought it not robbery to be equal with God:*

The enemy assignment is to kill, steal and destroy. So his greatest pleasure or gain is not only in the thief or robber it's actually greatest when he gets in the spirit of God's people, win a saint, take a Christian - that's victory hells development, the haters praise and party keeping them even hotter going seeking what lame weak soul he can remove from being saved. You have to have great faith, to believe and to trust and stand and remain. Getting there may not have been as hard as staying under God's covenant. Especially if we have those you think are the masses and you discover the **M** has been removed!!! This thing is painful. ***Proverbs 15:13*** *A merry heart maketh a cheerful countenance: but by sorrow of the heart the spirit is broken.* I would not want to see anybody lose their way in the kingdom. That agony and anguish of a bruised, battered and crushed spirit that doesn't seem to heal as fast as outer scars. Those that say they follow Jesus: well let's not take the power of God out of the church. We need to save more souls, lead people through sanctification, getting them deliverance and healing in the midst of their storms, trials and tribulations. Loving people is what God wants us to do-but He wants us to trust Him the more as we do this.

1 John 3:18 *Dear/ Little children, let us not love in word or talk/tongue but indeed and in truth.*

Not just with our mouths, what we say out of it, but LOVE is an action word what we do, how we respond, what we show, what we feel who we represent! There's an old song, "what the world needs now is love sweet love"!!! His truth is in His love!

FINAL INSTRUCTIONS

1 Thessalonians 5:12-17 Now we ask you, brothers and sisters, to acknowledge those who work hard among you, who care for you in the Lord and who admonish you. 13 Hold them in the highest regard in love because of their work. Live in peace with each other. 14 And we urge you, brothers and sisters, warn those who are idle and disruptive, encourage the disheartened, help the weak, be patient with everyone. 15 Make sure that nobody pays back wrong for wrong, but always strive to do what is good for each other and for everyone else. 16 Rejoice always, 17 pray continually,

Now we see it here as Paul puts it plain, as well we read ALL these wonderful glorious God given scriptures. From a child we are taught to read that reading is fundamental. It is; so very true My granddaughter has to read twenty minutes a night for school, and write a five-line summary of what the book was about and what she liked about the story. Well I see the beam in her eyes as she reads and gets excited about the fun and how sweet and nice the story was.

Well reading is fundamental indeed. BUT do you know that reading the bible is basic living for life - ministerial living. I am not talking about school nursery books and rhymes, fiction, and princess diaries, and happy endings that get children's eyes glowing and the excitement although that should be our reaction when we read the scriptures.

However, in the above scripture reading what do we take from that? The WORD is to urge us, admonish us, move us, enlighten us and the scriptures are given to us as Words to live by. We should model Christ and be an example of the goodness of Jesus, taste just how good the Lord is. See we can make the world a better place if we exercised His likeness. I enjoy being a Jesus promoter, a gospel educator, a love demonstrator, and a kingdom offering. It's a privilege being an ambassador for Christ, His representative and to have great urgency to see others move and do just so accordingly. Now I am fully aware of human urges-however, I have concern about God's urgency and there's an urgent call to populate and expand His kingdom. A call of humanity for the divinity. When we process this and understand His mankind, His mandate; there will be elevation in the body of Christ. That we band together and become one big puzzle fitting all pieces distinctly together with a uniqueness of Christian individuals with God given gifts that we figured it out and know where we ALL fit collectively and in unity. One big community of saints throughout our churches, nations, countries, and in the world. God's World.

Prophetic Principle Peace

Dynamic Deliverance

Desired Doctrine

Destined Destiny

Corrected Convocation

Contracted Convictions

Solid Saints

Saved Souls

Satisfied Sanctification

Relevant Revival

Revealed Restoration

Real Righteousness

Redefined Revelation

Renewed Redemption

Unique Universal Unity

Fascinated Father Faith

Humble Holiness

Consistent Constant Christ at the Cross

ALL for God's Great Glory!

Everybody wants an emoji – well emoji eternal and everlasting that's it!

We need to start making some Jesus geniuses and some "Jesus preneurs."

I don't understand how people going through ALL the motions up in the church hollering, praising, worshipping, shouting and even preaching, and they leave the church and even their true character in the church - have no demonstration of Christ. Doing all the emotions and acting with no manifestation. It's like they are not even ashamed of this before the Lord. How do you literally talk from the bible and walking in hell up in the church? Furthermore, be really careful how one somebody can cause this much spiritual abuse. Similar to just one crazy person making a lot of trouble for a lot of people. You all in yourself, teaching your very own 'YOU' version, like you are this church, you are the church, you the only member in this church. You act like this is your church, and what you want to do is the only thing that can be done and the only thing that will get done. Lord help us!

Proverbs 28:26 He that trusteth in his own heart/mind is a fool: but whoso walketh wisely/in wisdom, he shall/will be delivered.

Let me be honest and say that I actually felt embarrassed before the Lord on the account of the way others treated me. That's how it resulted in ministry shame, kingdom humiliation and spiritual rape. Like how do I live before the Spirit of this great God? And be subject to this spiritual abuse. My spirit was like it was on mute. BUT:

Psalm 147:3 He healeth the broken in heart, and bindeth up their wounds.

FINAL ANALYSIS

Philippians 4:8 Finally, brethren, whatsoever things are true, whatsoever things are honest, whatsoever things are just, whatsoever things are pure, whatsoever things are lovely, whatsoever things are of good report; if there be any virtue, and if there be any praise, think on these things.

Yes a very good analysis as this scripture is one of my favorites. Since we know God inspires and gives assurances as Paul writes to the Philippians. That no matter what! His goodness is what we need to focus on and think on. It's the peace that God gives us in everything we got going on. If we want to experience God's truth, we have to learn to take control of our thinking. When the enemy takes over your thinking you become the foolish, the idiots, the liars, the cheaters, the fornicators, the thinking of suicide, and bad habits thoughts to kill, rape, do drugs and abuse alcohol. No matter what our brain is thinking but it's our heart that follows Christ. That is our membership in one body in Christ. Everybody in the church is not a Christian no more than going to church makes you a Christian. Once you become a born-again Christian you simply chase after God, you are trying to run his race, you keep seeking, you keep searching, you want more and more; and it becomes your Christian lifestyle, your habits and your ways. Know Paul is exhorting/offering victory if we just think on these things the right things, the good things, and the things that bring about peace.

Now as the world revolves God's people are supposed to evolve. Times we are living in right now I will say that people in the world have developed a contrite spirit personally, professionally, corporately, and yes spiritually. That's why there's so much ungodly pain, mental ailments and breakdowns, our mind is suffering because the people of God are not capturing enough souls. I am praying for prosperity, but I am praying first that people just learn to live right. I know we can never change everybody I'm not that shallow minded-but I feel more people can be saved. It's such a spiritual warfare and a world war us going on and what can we do about it to help eliminate this crisis. If ISIS', minions and other gangs, terrorist and cults and unidentified martyrs can be recouped and growing what can we do to attract people in the Christian realm. Like I said we can never change and save everybody but only a few bodies. We need something to attract people minds. By walking around weary and worried all the time and seeing what they seeing we need to give them new sight, new revelation.

Churches cannot say they are a covenant and yet don't cover the people with God's true love. They can't say you a deliverance church and you dividing and deserting the people, you can't say your Baptist and you're bathing in mess and foolishness. You can't be Pentecostal and you perpetrating Christ. *Let's just be real here.* Even the replete of scriptures in the book of Acts teaches us our church history, its growth, it's our fellowship as believers, and it's a pattern and basic characteristics for us to live by and proclaim the WORD of the Lord being led by the Holy Spirit.

Acts 2:41-47 So those who received his word were baptized, and there were added that day about three thousand souls.

The Fellowship of the Believers

42 And they devoted themselves to the apostles' teaching and the fellowship, to the breaking of bread and the prayers. 43 And awe[a] came upon every soul, and many wonders and signs were being done through the apostles. 44 And all who believed were together and had all things in common. 45 And they were selling their possessions and belongings and distributing the proceeds to all, as any had need. 46 And day by day, attending the temple together and breaking bread in their homes, they received their food with glad and generous hearts, 47 praising God and having favor with all the people. And the Lord added to their number day by day those who were being saved.

Acts 16:5 So the churches were strengthened in the faith and grew daily in numbers.

Acts 17:11 Now the Berean Jews were of more noble character than those in Thessalonica, for they received the message with great eagerness and examined the Scriptures every day to see if what Paul said was true.

I am not talking about any church I'm just using as example that the division and separation and coming apart and falling and breaking into pieces has got to stop. We can't have outreach ministries and you're chasing people out. Come on is all I'm saying. We have to find a better way. Church by church, nation by nation country by country, community by community. So, I don't care how many churches is on one block how many people are coming you have ten members, the one up the street has a hundred. The one on the corner got a thousand. Well we still got a billion uncharted, lost, sick, unsaved and dying. A house divided will never stand. I know my experience; I'm not alone and you can believe this word too:

Isaiah 40:28-30 Have you not known? Have you not heard?
The LORD is the everlasting God, the Creator of the ends of the earth.
He does not faint or grow weary; his understanding is unsearchable.
29 He gives power to the faint, and to him who has no might he increases strength. 30 Even youths shall faint and be weary, and young men shall fall exhausted/utterly fall
31 but they who wait for the LORD shall renew their strength; they shall mount up with wings like eagles; they shall run and not be weary; they shall walk and not faint.

When you learn that everyone in the church is not saved is one thing; but when you got people going and showing up running the church Sunday after Sunday and all during the week and never miss the church doors being opened and think they got Jesus' attention and Heaven is definite – I wonder what spirit they're under? And pay so much attention to you what is their true intention. How do they not know just how real God is! He's not a toy you pick up and turn on and play with as you want when you want. Like the toy this Christmas it's your favorite and by end of January, you no longer play with it or perhaps you broke it! And just can't play with it. This is not a game. Isaiah tells us HE IS OUR ONLY SAVIOR.

Isaiah 43 Israel's Only Savior
*But now thus says the L*ORD*, he who created you, O Jacob, he who formed you, O Israel: "Fear not, for I have redeemed you; I have called you by name, you are mine.2 When you pass through the waters, I will be with you;*
*and through the rivers, they shall not overwhelm you; when you walk through fire you shall not be burned, and the flame shall not consume you. 3 For I am the L*ORD *your God, the Holy One of Israel, your Savior.*

And since He is the only savior, I need insurance on my soul. So, I am going to live right now, not later, I am not going to wait I want assurance now! And that is only provided at His will as you choose to live. Repentance is accountancy, love is accountability, living right is our responsibility since the Holy Spirit enables us. Be certain that when he comes, He's coming back as this tells us:

Ephesians 5:26-27 That he might sanctify and cleanse it with the washing of water by the word,27 That he might present it to himself a glorious church, not having spot, or wrinkle, or any such thing; but that it should be holy and without blemish.

Get out of the church trying to castrate, cripple, crush, crumble, crucify, leaving people with critical spirits that you cursed them in your words, deeds and actions. Trampling those that are already wounded, pouring salt on those injuries instead of being the SALT of the earth, hurting those that are hurt, leaving them terminally ill in their spirits. After all that was done for us. God has crafted us to be His masterpiece. His workmanship and we are supposed to be an example not an imposter e. We are not counterfeit of the true Holy Spirit we are the righteous living with the Holy Spirit.

2 Timothy 2:15 Study to shew thyself approved unto God, a workman that needeth not to be ashamed, rightly dividing the word of truth.

Study the Word and then be a living, breathing, walking, talking, example of this great God. His Word is nourishment for our bodies, its food to feed us daily. The essential goodness of God is in ALL creation. So, we can never ever separate Him from His creation. He is the great creator of everything and ALL things.

One More thing

God is a conceited God-as He should be! He knows what He can do and he knows He's ALL that! Yes, an absolute Christ can do anything. Bet He knows He's bout it about it and very sure and confident of it!!! As well God is a jealous God. Let me share one of His many great attributes: That our God is most compassionate; the passion/compassion of Christ is who He is through and through. I can write another 100 plus chapters on His compassion alone. I would not want to leave out the scriptures on just how compassionate our God ultimately is. But I will leave you with one:

1 Peter 3:8-17 Amplified Bible (AMP)
8 Finally, all of you be like-minded [united in spirit], sympathetic, brotherly, kindhearted [courteous and compassionate toward each other as members of one household], and humble in spirit; 9 and never return evil for evil or insult for insult [avoid scolding, berating, and any kind of abuse], but on the contrary, give a blessing [pray for one another's well-being, contentment, and protection]; for you have been called for this very purpose, that you might inherit a blessing [from God that brings well-being, happiness, and protection]. 10 For,

"THE ONE WHO WANTS TO ENJOY LIFE AND SEE GOOD DAYS [good—whether apparent or not],
MUST KEEP HIS TONGUE FREE FROM EVIL AND HIS LIPS FROM SPEAKING GUILE (treachery, deceit).
11 "HE MUST TURN AWAY FROM WICKEDNESS AND DO WHAT IS RIGHT.

HE MUST SEARCH FOR PEACE [with God, with self, with others] AND PURSUE IT EAGERLY[actively—not merely desiring it].

12 "FOR THE EYES OF THE LORD ARE [looking favorably] UPON THE RIGHTEOUS (the upright), AND HIS EARS ARE ATTENTIVE TO THEIR PRAYER (eager to answer), BUT THE FACE OF THE LORD IS AGAINST THOSE WHO PRACTICE EVIL."

13 Now who is there to hurt you if you become enthusiastic for what is good? 14 But even if you should suffer for the sake of righteousness [though it is not certain that you will], you are still blessed [happy, to be admired and favored by God]. DO NOT BE AFRAID OF THEIR INTIMIDATING THREATS, NOR BE TROUBLED or DISTURBED [by their opposition]. 15 But in your hearts set Christ apart [as holy—acknowledging Him, giving Him first place in your lives] as Lord. Always be ready to give a [logical] defense to anyone who asks you to account for the hope and confident assurance [elicited by faith] that is within you, yet [do it] with gentleness and respect. 16 And see to it that your conscience is entirely clear, so that every time you are slandered or falsely accused, those who attack or disparage your good behavior in Christ will be shamed [by their own words]. 17 For it is better that you suffer [unjustly] for doing what is right, if that should be God's will, than [to suffer justly] for doing wrong.

I chose to share the amplified version as to give full understanding. As I mentioned the scriptures are replete, we are inundated with them both in the OLD and the NEW

Testaments. **Our God is first, compassionate.** That just identifies Him and to speak one word of who He is.

As well we need to keep cliques out of the church – cliques form for no good reasons other than to stir up trouble, start mess, cause confusion, make chaos and bring hurt. I come from a time when we had crews! So, what we need is *Christian crews!* People down for you, people helping you, rock with you, roll with and are there for you, we about serving the same God! You down with GOD yeah you know me!!! Christian crews hang and holla! – While these cliques want to harm and hurt!

ME

To identify myself let me explain I am not perfect as I said. True, I have been a saint, a Christian [Still], a God fearing, Jesus joy, a Holy Spirit celebrator, a heart for God, and His love. AND I have been a victim of church hurt! I know what happened to me I am not the first nor will I be the last. I am not the only one. Others may even think maybe it's her! And I will not argue or dispute that because we ALL have opinions.

But in my heart of hearts I know what I faced, what was done, what I received and I know that this warfare of unkind, non-kingdom non righteous behavior stimulated and exercised in my presence and witnessed before me is MY church hurt! Believe me when I say with the love of Christ that died for you and I, this was only because people are living with envy, insecurities, and jealousy and title trips of power. Leverage, that given the ability and authority to exercise it according to their will and their way. Well, they are going to act and enforce it and you have to take it and move on and deal with your hurt OR rather you move in silence, suffer in silence or decide to speak about it. Spiritual attacks are real!

Dealing with this is a new dimension another level kind of hurt a different kind of pain. Like what medicine from heaven corrects, fix and heal this. "HIS WORD!" Hard, difficult, much tried, testing, aggravating, frustrating, spiritual debilitating. Yes! That word is life, the restoration, the salvation, the help. That if it was not for the power of prayer, that word that's a strong tower. I don't know where I would be… I then read a great quote:

"In the shadow of my hurt, forgiveness feels like a decision to reward my enemy. But in the shadow of the cross, forgiveness is merely a gift from one undeserving soul to another."
— Andy Stanley

Me as forgiving as I am, OH MY GOD, to confirm one of the reasons I am saved-I preached on forgiveness ask people that know me I am one of the most forgiving compassionate people Seriously! I walk in forgiveness, I show forgiveness, and I live in forgiveness. Forgiveness is powerful, there's strength, freedom and peace in forgiveness, Jesus is the perfect example of forgiveness. OUR GOD FIRST FORGAVE US! YET another example of our God!!!! AND the scriptures are yet again, replete! BUT let's just go with the ultimate plea from the cross:

And Jesus said, "Father, forgive them, for they know not what they do." And they cast lots to divide his garments. **Luke 23:34**

That after hours of agony, pain, suffering, belligerent beatings being nailed to the cross - whipped, tortured, tormented physically beyond recognition. Blood streaming down His face and everywhere, relentless, senseless brutality. They even pierced Him in His sides with stakes and thorns and placed a horned crown on His head – which this unimaginable, unthinkable, despicable act, how He must have felt the strife and the sacrifice something no one humanly possible can withstand, or fulfill. Punished for all the crimes HE NEVER even committed. That this ruthless ordeal. This awkward beating, awful crucifixion the most devastating death in history. *He still uttered instructions to forgive...*

Another interesting quote:

"As leaders, we are never responsible for filling anyone else's cup. Our responsibility is to empty ours."
— Andy Stanley, Deep and Wide: Creating Churches Unchurched People Love to Attend

Here's a quote, **'everyone in church is not of the gospel.'** So, I must express my true desires. Yes-empty my cup but when you look to always be filled and since I am a worshipper, and a seeker and I am one who forever praises, and I yearn to be taught I desire more than anything to be shepherded. I believe in being under someone's profound, prolific tutelage. I'm chasing for kingdom, building, growing and expansion. I cannot turn away from this, I will not walk or run away from this! I yearn to be poured into and to pour out. I am open, I have visions I will follow a visionary that is according to God's orchestrated plan, I not blindly following I am spiritually following. I sought the Lord and He heard my cries, He delivered me from my fears. I need to be encouraged, motivated, supported and pushed as well. I am not stubborn I'm eager an ALL-time seeker, and I want to be taught and trained. I want that guidance, structure I can preach a word, I live by the word-BUT I WANT TO HAVE THAT ABILITY TO REMAIN. I must have that covering as my spirit sought and yearns to be under somebody. That's what a leader shows us. Great leaders make leaders. Create other disciples. I want to follow that Shepherd on Gods Highway. Or I'm going no way at ALL!!! A leader to chaperone me and elevate me and pick me up when I am falling and to help keep me from slipping – My Spirits are no longer cremated they are still very much alive. Bursting and blazing for the fire and glory of God!

Revelation 21:8 But the fearful, and unbelieving, and the abominable, and murderers, and whoremongers, and sorcerers, and idolaters, and all liars, shall have their part in the lake which burneth with fire and brimstone: which is the second death.

This scripture is the danger my spirits were in. BUT I knew I wasn't created to fit in but to stand out! No way was I going to let the devil have his way. Tribulation came my way but I was not letting any bully, any beast turns me away. Yes! Keep me from the altered worship that was taking place anyway! But not purge and forge my spirits into controversy. NO! I am anointed to win! Winners never quit and quitters never win. I had to take self-control we know the spirit is tempted, but I was not for the condemnation, the contamination, or the damnation of my soul being at the hands of man. Looking like I put more in man than God because I was going after something and someone that didn't accept me!

My spirits had been kidnapped they were hijacked and taking hostage-guess what? I was getting it back and taking it back by the power of the Holy Spirit that is within me. I was not letting no Devil in hell take me out! I wasn't a practiced praise leader, or a rehearsed worshipper-I was a diehard Christian in heart, I knew the master of my soul, the captain of my ship! And YES! I was even that BITCH-*Bet I'm That Christ Hoe!* I'm not dealing with pimping pulpits that is of the flesh; But *ohhh* Christ can pimp me out ALL day, any day in and every which way, I will do just what He says, what He needs and exactly what He wants! Because MY BIBLE TELLS ME SO!!! I am sold out for Christ! I'm just kicking facts of truth. RE: "ME." Dealing with the agony, the weight on my shoulder you feel like you no longer carrying your cross but it dropped out from under you. Salvaged and ruptured spirits eating me inside out, and to stay was like outside in. I don't wish this on anybody, I fervently pray that it's not something contagious, but I feel others are experiencing it! Keeping silence and withdrawn from speaking of it and talking about it. We need to watch, be mindful Christ minded and be careful especially of those with leadership authority of how we treat parishioners, because everyone is not as strong in mind, body and soul. The spirits are tried, they are tested, the Devil is clever and strategically runs interference that the interruption will kill you! I'm serious. This is detrimental to our salvation. Don't let your spirits get twisted, mangled, tangled and scrambled. We have a straightway to Christ! So, know that my leaving was to save myself.

Praise be to God I was wising up to know it's not a crime to be forsaken by man! My Jesus was forsaken on the cross! Even David asked why you are casting down on my soul. And Isaiah let me know it will be Ok anyhow.

Isaiah 49:13-16

13 *Sing for joy, O heavens, and exult, O earth;*
 break forth, O mountains, into singing!
For the LORD *has comforted his people*
 and will have compassion on his afflicted.

14 *But Zion said, "The* LORD *has forsaken me;*
 my Lord has forgotten me."

15 *"Can a woman forget her nursing child,*
 that she should have no compassion on the son of her womb?
Even these may forget,
 yet I will not forget you.
16 *Behold, I have engraved you on the palms of my hands;*
 your walls are continually before me.

Everything just becomes centered on God. It's good, everything is Him. That's why we know His Word and take Him at his WORD! Trust and Believe His Word.

When I went through rejection and was ignoring it – well it became mental abuse. I was not aware at first that my rejection was a blessing. But in the beginning, I was experiencing a spiritual meltdown. I didn't see a breakthrough-I was literally breaking down. Like WOW! [Worthless oh women] I don't exist! The Devil is a liar. The following descriptors capture my emotions: defeat, deceit, depression, oppression, denial, self-destruction, omission, opposition, spirit demolition, anguish, mental unstable, spiritual delinquent, spiritually frustration, kingdom aggravation, ministry humiliation, congregational shame, pulpit bitterness, a loafer and a scoffer mindset, a ill church attitude, a lost soul, spiritual damnation, ministry misery, having feeling some monster spiritual beast trying to consume me and be my every thought.

Two spiritual powers, one literally destroying me and the other trying to prevent me. I had to be still, listen and act on that Holy Spiritual of great prevention. That spirit that preserves, that keeps that prevails. I was heading in a danger zone, but praise be to God! My spirits surrendered to the voice tarrying with me. No longer confused by the enemy's thoughts.

I was in a place that I was not sure where I was at! BUT I felt I didn't belong there. AND I was reminded of his word. I came out and believe me you too will come out! God gives us that assurance in His Word. See you will never understand how much hurt I really felt or experienced unless it's happened to you! And you must stand on every encouraging, every empowered, every instruction, every word of the Lord! Scriptures are doctrine for us to live by.

Romans 8:38-39 *For I am sure that neither death nor life, nor angels nor rulers, nor things present nor things to come, nor powers, 39 nor height nor depth, nor anything* *else in all creation, will be able to separate us from the love of God in Christ Jesus our Lord.*

*I will leave you with this about me again!

I will not be fooled, misguided, misdirected or misled by anybody ever as long as I am saved, sanctified, living and breathing. Seriously, know that any person will have to wake up in B.C. to fool, trick or pull a wool or anything over me. And I don't ever see that happening... and further more since it's truly impossible for anybody to wake up before Christ - I KNOW THAT'S NOT HAPPENING!!!

CONCLUSION PART I

My battle, my injustice, my challenge, my interference, my anger, my defeat, my pain, my suffering, my, shame, my humiliation, my disruption, my burden, my assault, my assassination, my invasion, my being derailed, my disengagement, my disenfranchised, my disintegration, my loss, my drainage, my sabotage, my ill feelings, my dismay, my distraught, my damage, my disgrace, my abandonment, and my ungodly treatment;: these are all euphemisms for the moments and the treatments I received in real-life.

Well that God that pulls you out over every low valley, bring you across wild rivers, that God that keep you through the midst of every storm, and takes you over every mountain; that God that promises to never leave you or forsake you, that God that sent His only begotten Son, who died and rose for us, He shed His blood for us, the one that lives in us, the El-Ohim that God is always with us-in season and out, day and night, night and day, every year, every month, every week, every moment, every day, every minute, every second, and every breath that remains in us even after we have taken our last breath. That God!

Well when you know that manipulation can never overtake manifestation, you have assurance that God is ALL! We must understand there will be ministry misfits. They need to stop crawling up in the churches and sabotaging Gods work will and His people. But praise be to God we live in the overflow, we become victorious and overcome. That's how I was able to **turn** my **hurt** around! By hearing - **Having Unction Righteous Truth...**

***Deuteronomy 30:1-14** The Message (MSG)*
1-5 Here's what will happen. While you're out among the nations where GOD has dispersed you and the blessings and curses come in just the way I have set them before you, and you and your children take them seriously and come back to GOD, your God, and obey him with your whole heart and soul according to everything that I command you today, **GOD, your God, will restore everything you lost;** *he'll have compassion on you; he'll come back and pick up the pieces from all the places where you were scattered. No matter how far away you end up, GOD, your God, will get you out of there and bring you back to the land your ancestors once possessed. It will be yours again. He will give you a good life and make you more numerous than your ancestors.*

6-7 GOD, your God, will cut away the thick calluses on your heart and your children's hearts, freeing you to love GOD, your God, with your whole heart and soul and live, really live. GOD, your God, will put all these curses on your enemies who hated you and were out to get you.

8-9 And you will make a new start, listening obediently to GOD, keeping all his commandments that I'm commanding you today. GOD, your God, will outdo himself in making things go well for you: you'll have babies, get calves, grow crops, and enjoy an all-around good life. Yes, GOD will start enjoying you again, making things go well for you just as he enjoyed doing it for your ancestors.

10 But only if you listen obediently to GOD, your God, and keep the commandments and regulations written in this Book of Revelation. Nothing halfhearted here; you must return to GOD, your God, totally, heart and soul, holding nothing back.

11-14 This commandment that I'm commanding you today isn't too much for you, it's not out of your reach. It's not on a high mountain—you don't have to get mountaineers to climb the peak and bring it down to your level and explain it before you can live it. And it's not across the ocean—you don't have to send sailors out to get it, bring it back, and then explain it before you can live it. No. The word is right here and now—as near as the tongue in your mouth, as near as the heart in your chest. Just do it!

Note: the scripture starts off with **'here's what will happen.'** WELL guess what? That's what happened the reason I was able to leave, and remove myself. God's mantle and His manifestation is the greatest.

During that process and transition it was well with my soul. I felt that from God. The Holy Spirit took me out to remain within. I had to realize that and operate accordingly. The struggle was over, the test was final exam, and I existed!

Kingdom forgiveness, my life in the church. God restores an offended Christian even in the worst of their hurt. In the midst of every storm no matter who's wrong, what went wrong, how wrong, or for how long? He mends, He binds, He fixes, He restores, and He revives us to that place of righteous peace.

Matthew 18:21-22 Then Peter came to Jesus and asked, "Lord, how many times shall I forgive my brother or sister who sins against me? Up to seven times?" 22 Jesus answered, "I tell you, not seven times, but seventy-seven times.

We live wholly on mercy and forgiveness. The truth Jesus is telling us, we are to forgive as many times as it takes. I need you ALL to understand that I have forgiven, I have forgiveness in my heart, I've been a forgiveness candidate since I became saved. I made the choice during a period in my life where I was torn and it was not about forgiving because that part was already done. It was about being torn into two and knowing how to choose, make a decision and pray that it's of God. Because even as you forgive – you need to understand the actions and levels of the other side of those that you have forgiven. The difference is your forgiveness is always for self. BUT your forgiveness is not foolishness.

I'll explain- just because they continue to come to church don't mean that they have come to Christ! God prepared me not to go back so that I can continuously forgive them in advance. Because my return, my presence, my going back will not change them. I have been through the same responses and actions for a very long time. When you are dealing with insecurities, envy and idolatries those traits are a dangerous stronghold. And the spirit of jealousy is an insult to God first and foremost.

The saints must stop being **secret servants** in the church and serving when convenient and only for certain leaders. That's not the way to do church. *you a secret server, not a true servant,* or fruitful-instead you're full of falsehood and false teachings. Your doctrine is dangerous to the kingdom. Keeping schemes and fornicating Gods work for self-gratification. You are satisfying your messy flesh. Stop coming to church every Sunday and running out Gods people with this church mockery and foolery. Taking titles, giving titles, some are called some are chosen and you are part of those **that just went.** Coming to church every time the doors open but you are 'churching' others out while doors on them. The evilness and being hell raisers. Satan's sanctuary practice preachers and promoters. How can we stop church attacks with Pit Bulls sitting in the pulpits?

Romans 14:13-17 Therefore let us not pass judgment on one another any longer, but rather decide never to put a stumbling block or hindrance in the way of a brother. I know and am persuaded in the Lord Jesus that nothing is unclean in itself, but it is unclean for anyone who thinks it unclean. For if your brother is grieved by what you eat, you are no longer walking in love. By what you eat, do not destroy the one for whom Christ died. So do not let what you regard as good be spoken of as evil. For the kingdom of God is not a matter of eating and drinking but of righteousness and peace and joy in the Holy Spirit.

I told myself even in my sorrow, life is to live and never give up but remember to live and look up - as long as I wake up!

Just as trees lose every leaf it still stands planted and wait for the next season. I want to be like a tree planted by the rivers still standing even in adversity. I am reminded in

Jeremiah 17:8 He is like a tree planted by water, that sends out its roots by the stream, and does not fear when heat comes, for its leaves remain green, and is not anxious in the year of drought, for it does not cease to bear fruit."

Those filled with temptation as those that are untamable, the cliques and the groupies in the church that still think team is spelled with an "I" and don't know what it means for ministry collaboration. That's on them! Because man may hurt you-But the Lord God is Alpha and Omega, He is the beginning and the end. So only God can draw me to my soul salvation. Not haters, agitators, instigators and fornicators. I am not about to be confused in ministry madness. And my brothers and sisters you shouldn't be either. We have a remedy and a resolution His name is Jesus and it's written in His Father's Word…He will resolve any matters of the heart!!! For you and me. He will make your enemies your footstool. you can keep on moving and keep on stepping. That God will replenish, nourish and restore that **spiritual drought** you were in.

Look where in *__John 15:1-7__* **it says:**

"I am the true vine, and my Father is the gardener. 2 He cuts off every branch in me that bears no fruit, while every branch that does bear fruit he prunes so that it will be even more fruitful. 3 You are already clean because of the word I have spoken to you. 4 Remain in me, as I also remain in you. No branch can bear fruit by itself; it must remain in the vine. Neither can you bear fruit unless you remain in me.

5 "I am the vine; you are the branches. If you remain in me and I in you, you will bear much fruit; apart from me you can do nothing. 6 If you do not remain in me, you are like a branch that is thrown away and withers; such branches are picked up, thrown into the fire and burned. 7 If you remain in me and my words remain in you, ask whatever you wish, and it will be done for you.

Verse 5 in the KJV says: *for without me ye can do nothing.*

And that's right; ***Without Him, we can do nothing, we are nothing without Him!***

PART II

My earnest plea is that the churches grow the kingdom, build and God's people be delivered. We are supposed to grow in grace, grow in Christ, produce, save and win souls. Remove hurt from our hearts and remove it out of the churches and help one another the way God has so ordered. *Reclaiming the name of Jesus.* Coming to church being a pew warmer because of the haters that play church and can sing a hymn but don't know Him; or directing a choir and have not receive the Lord's direction for themselves.

Hebrews 6:1 Therefore let us leave the elementary doctrine of Christ and go on to maturity, not laying again a foundation of repentance from dead works and of faith toward God,

I just love this scripture-

2 Corinthians 13:11 Finally, brothers, rejoice. Aim for restoration, comfort one another, agree with one another, live in peace; and the God of love and peace will be with you.

Hear what Paul is telling us *'live in peace; and the God of love and peace will be with you.'* We read this and yet and still want to hurt people. {I heard that hurt people hurt people}. There's truth to that and then there are those that hurt others because they can deal easier of a messy flesh that serves their underlying ungodly malicious ways. Simply don't want to see anybody else happy or striving- that selfish, insecure, envy spirit consumes and controls them. In ***Psalms*** it tells us *the Lord test the righteous and the wicked but he hates the violent, the lawless, the wicked and the cruel with a passion.*

For those that don't want to cooperate and celebrate the passionate Christ, that's on them…. I count myself as value to God! I am not about to be berated into the Devil's Den. God's people need to start being the majority and not the minority in this business of the kingdom. Being about Our Father's business. We need to be our brothers and our sister's keepers in the kingdom.

James 2:1-4 *My brothers, show no partiality as you hold the faith in our Lord Jesus Christ, the Lord of glory. For if a man wearing a gold ring and fine clothing comes into your assembly, and a poor man in shabby clothing also comes in, and if you pay attention to the one who wears the fine clothing and say, "You sit here in a good place," while you say to the poor man, "You stand over there," or, "Sit down at my feet," have you not then made distinctions among yourselves and become judges with evil thoughts?*

Once you have buried the Word in you along with all your sins, uncleanness, hatred, no good deeds, follies and woes, you are no longer intimidated, paranoid, or part of Satan's solitary confinement. You are content with the master. You serve period. You don't serve with a question mark; no need to doubt, hesitate or procrastinate. Those things hinder and stop the process. We must be the Jesus' recruiters, ready to recruit more souls, and save people from their sins, pain, agony, strife, and struggles they face in life. We still have people sick, dying, homeless, jobless, without families, killing, suffering and self-destructing.

The Devil is devious, deceitful, detrimental, cleaver, strategic, manipulative, deceiving, disoriented, conniving, psychotic, frightful and a liar. His aggressiveness will infiltrate you if you don't stand ground and keep the Word of God in you, believing, trusting and always remain faithful.

PART III

Revelation 3:7 *"And to the angel of the church in Philadelphia write: 'The words of the holy one, the true one, who has the key of David, who opens and no one will shut, who shuts and no one opens.*

Stop closing doors on God's people shutting them out, bashing and disregarding them because you have little power and some authority. ONLY GOD has ALL authority and He's certainly ALL POWERFUL.

See those that are passive aggressive and have big egos will throw their weight around on those they feel are beneath them or of course powerless. Of course, you remember the bully on the playground; their life becomes this playground. . . [That's ok, because if serving is beneath you then certainly leadership is beyond you-*that explains it*]. BUT PLEASE we have to stop pulpit bullies and leadership bullying. There's NO PRAISE IN THAT! In Fact, there is not even glory in that! All you got is a self-praise that only those who are subordinate, puppeteers, protégé phonies, flunkies, false prophets, non-witnesses, devils counsel, fake followers celebrate your eradicated actions. There's no God in that! That's all you, and it's very foolish.

Proverbs 1:7 The fear of the LORD is the beginning of knowledge; fools despise wisdom and instruction.

I need to add that the bible is also outlined with countless scriptures for those that hurt other body of believers: I'll share a few more but you can open your bible and read these exhortations. I know this hurt is a serious thing and it's because of those who are unteachable and unapproachable because they have not come to Christ they are not saved. Their souls are not truly delivered from facets of the world. They have studied the bible but have not comprehended God's Word fully and they are not Christ ambassadors or representatives but Satan sowers.

Luke 17:1-2 And he said to his disciples, "Temptations to sin are sure to come, but woe to the one through whom they come! It would be better for him if a millstone were hung around his neck and he were cast into the sea than that he should cause one of these little ones to sin.

I love these two

Galatians 2:20 I have been crucified with Christ. It is no longer I who live, but Christ who lives in me. And the life I now live in the flesh I live by faith in the Son of God, who loved me and gave himself for me.

John 15:18-19 "If the world hates you, know that it has hated me before it hated you. If you were of the world, the world would love you as its own; but because you are not of the world, but I chose you out of the world, therefore the world hates you.

And in Matthew 7 It is really broken down for our understanding and interpretation.

Matthew 7

Judging Others

"Judge not, that you be not judged. 2 For with the judgment you pronounce you will be judged, and with the measure you use it will be measured to you. 3 Why do you see the speck that is in your brother's eye, but do not notice the log that is in your own eye? 4 Or how can you say to your brother, 'Let me take the speck out of your eye,' when there is the log in your own eye? 5 You hypocrite, first take the log out of your own eye, and then you will see clearly to take the speck out of your brother's eye.

6 "Do not give dogs what is holy, and do not throw your pearls before pigs, lest they trample them underfoot and turn to attack you.

Ask, and It Will Be Given

7 "Ask, and it will be given to you; seek, and you will find; knock, and it will be opened to you. 8 For everyone who asks receives, and the one who seeks finds, and to the one who knocks it will be opened. 9 Or which one of you, if his son asks him for bread, will give him a stone? 10 Or if he asks for a fish, will give him a serpent? 11 If you then, who are evil, know how to give good gifts to your children, how much more will your Father who is in heaven give good things to those who ask him!

The Golden Rule

12 *"So whatever you wish that others would do to you, do also to them, for this is the Law and the Prophets.*

13 *"Enter by the narrow gate. For the gate is wide and the way is easy[a] that leads to destruction, and those who enter by it are many.* 14 *For the gate is narrow and the way is hard that leads to life, and those who find it are few.*

A Tree and Its Fruit

15 *"Beware of false prophets, who come to you in sheep's clothing but inwardly are ravenous wolves.* 16 *You will recognize them by their fruits. Are grapes gathered from thornbushes, or figs from thistles?* 17 *So, every healthy tree bears good fruit, but the diseased tree bears bad fruit.* 18 *A healthy tree cannot bear bad fruit, nor can a diseased tree bear good fruit.* 19 *Every tree that does not bear good fruit is cut down and thrown into the fire.* 20 *Thus you will recognize them by their fruits.*

I Never Knew You

21 *"Not everyone who says to me, 'Lord, Lord,' will enter the kingdom of heaven, but the one who does the will of my Father who is in heaven.* 22 *On that day many will say to me, 'Lord, Lord, did we not prophesy in your name, and cast out demons in your name, and do many mighty works in your name?'* 23 *And then will I declare to them, 'I never knew you; depart from me, you workers of lawlessness.'*

Build Your House on the Rock

24 *"Everyone then who hears these words of mine and does them will be like a wise man who built his house on the rock. 25 And the rain fell, and the floods came, and the winds blew and beat on that house, but it did not fall, because it had been founded on the rock. 26 And everyone who hears these words of mine and does not do them will be like a foolish man who built his house on the sand. 27 And the rain fell, and the floods came, and the winds blew and beat against that house, and it fell, and great was the fall of it."*

The Authority of Jesus

28 *And when Jesus finished these sayings, the crowds were astonished at his teaching, 29 for he was teaching them as one who had authority, and not as their scribes.*

Who's teachable and who's approachable, who are the spectators and dictators – BUT are not Christ demonstrators and laborers. How do we have leaders with passive aggressive attitudes and say they servants and saved. We cannot be unhinged Christians. We cannot be so dispositional that we destroy the fellowship, ruining relationships, make those that come to church like a homeless that they become churchless, that your qualifications and ability as a leader is beyond repair. That is not so!

1 Corinthians 6:9-11 Know ye not that the unrighteous shall not inherit the kingdom of God? Be not deceived:

*neither fornicators, nor idolaters, nor adulterers, nor
effeminate, nor abusers of themselves with mankind,
10 Nor thieves, nor covetous, nor drunkards, nor revilers,
nor extortioners, shall inherit the kingdom of God.
11 And such were some of you: but ye are washed, but ye
are sanctified, but ye are justified in the name of the Lord
Jesus, and by the Spirit of our God.*

Sinless perfection is impossible in this life, but our hatred
for sin becomes greater as we mature. I am distressed over
how much sin still exists as well as how much our people
are hurting. These actions of continuously doing things to
others that are not of God is identifying people as not being
redeemed by Christ. Being a Christian is having the ability
to fight against what is evil and overcome. Not to be
overturned, overtaken and overthrown by others with
higher authority. Know: Pit bulls have no place in the
church pulpit.

Flesh control is a stronghold! Not having the Holy Spirit,
these do not inherit the kingdom of God and naturally you
practice the works of the flesh.

Life through the Spirit is found in **Romans 8:1-5** *Therefore,
there is now no condemnation for those who are in Christ
Jesus, 2 because through Christ Jesus the law of the Spirit
who gives life has set you [a]free from the law of sin and
death. 3 For what the law was powerless to do because it
was weakened by the flesh, [b] God did by sending his own
Son in the likeness of sinful flesh to be a sin offering. [c] And
so he condemned sin in the flesh, 4 in order that the
righteous requirement of the law might be fully met in us,
who do not live according to the flesh but according to the
Spirit.   5 Those*

who live according to the flesh have their minds set on what the flesh desires; but those who live in accordance with the Spirit have their minds set on what the Spirit desires.

And it's made crystal clear to us here in **Galatians 5:19-21** *Now the works of the flesh are evident, which are: adultery, fornication, uncleanness, lewdness, idolatry, sorcery, hatred, contentions, jealousies, outbursts of wrath, selfish ambitions, dissensions, heresies, envy, murders, drunkenness, revelries, and the like; of which I tell you beforehand, just as I also told you in time past, that those who practice such things will not inherit the kingdom of God.*

Made clear again in **Ephesians 5:5-7** *For this you know, that no fornicator, unclean person, nor covetous man, who is an idolater, has any inheritance in the kingdom of Christ and God. Let no one deceive you with empty words, for because of these things the wrath of God comes upon the sons of disobedience. Therefore do not be partakers with them.*

How Timothy puts it plain: *But we know that the law is good if one uses it lawfully, knowing this: that the law is not made for a righteous (just) person, but for the lawless and insubordinate [disobedient], for the ungodly and for sinners, for the unholy and profane, for murderers of fathers and murderers of mothers, for manslayers (menstealers) (for liars), for fornicators, for sodomites, for kidnappers, for liars, for perjurers, and if there is any other thing that is contrary to sound doctrine. 1 Timothy 1:8-10*

Some versions call them lawbreakers and rebels, the sexually immoral, those that promise not to lie and do, as well steal. It's just all devilish acts and ways. Do we need to be reminded that - *Being righteous is just being right with God?*

Those described by this list are ones who continued in these activities without repentance. In writing to the church at Corinth, Paul emphasizes the forgiveness which remains available for the godless in this age of grace, if they would but turn to God in faith and be cleansed of their sin:

A Give it to God Scripture is found in ***Deuteronomy 6:13-14*** *"You shall fear the LORD your **God**. You shall serve him and hold fast to him, and by his name you shall swear. He is your praise. He is your **God**, who has done for you these great and terrifying things that your eyes have seen."*

The below seven (7) scriptures describe discord, dissension, division and separation among the body of Christians and within the church.

Acts 15:1-5 *Some men came down from Judea and began teaching the brethren, "Unless you are circumcised according to the custom of Moses, you cannot be saved." And when Paul and Barnabas had great dissension and debate with them, the brethren determined that Paul and Barnabas and some others of them should go up to Jerusalem to the apostles and elders concerning this issue. Therefore, being sent on their way by the church, they were passing through both Phoenicia and Samaria, describing in detail the conversion of the Gentiles, and were bringing great joy to all the brethren.*

Romans 16:17 *Now I urge you, brethren, keep your eye on those who cause dissensions and hindrances contrary to the teaching which you learned, and turn away from them.*

1 Corinthians 1:10-13 *Now I exhort you, brethren, by the name of our Lord Jesus Christ, that you all agree and that there be no divisions among you, but that you be made complete in the same mind and in the same judgment. For I have been informed concerning you, my brethren, by Chloe's people, that there are quarrels among you. Now I mean this, that each one of you is saying, "I am of Paul," and "I of Apollos," and "I of Cephas," and "I of Christ."read more.*

1 Corinthians 3:3 *for you are still fleshly. For since there is jealousy and strife among you, are you not fleshly, and are you not walking like mere men?*

1 Corinthians 6:1 *Does any one of you, when he has a case against his neighbor, dare to go to law before the unrighteous and not before the saints?*

1 Corinthians 11:18 *For, in the first place, when you come together as a church, I hear that divisions exist among you; and in part I believe it.*

Philippians 3:2 *Beware of the dogs, beware of the evil workers, beware of the false circumcision.*

1 John 2:19 *They went out from us, but they were not really of us; for if they had been of us, they would have remained with us; but they went out, so that it would be shown that they all are not of us.*

CHURCH CORRECTION

Romans 12:1-3 *I beseech you therefore, brethren, by the mercies of God, that ye present your bodies a living sacrifice, holy, acceptable unto God, which is your reasonable service.*
2 And be not conformed to this world: but be ye transformed by the renewing of your mind, that ye may prove what is that good, and acceptable, and perfect, will of God.

3 For I say, through the grace given unto me, to every man that is among you, not to think of himself more highly than he ought to think; but to think soberly, according as God hath dealt to every man the measure of faith.

This is the scripture in which Paul admonishes us, he urges us and set it straight as to we have an obligation to surrender and serve most appropriately. I love this how we are to be part of God's service and not of the world. It's like having a Jesus contract! We should all be prepared to sign it: this is a lifetime contract and comes with a guarantee. As well there are penalties and consequences if you break it. But we should all sign and enter the contract and agree to his commandments.

John 17:11 I will remain in the world no longer, but they are still in the world, and I am coming to you. Holy Father, protect them by the power of your name, the name you gave me, so that they may be one as we are one.

When you really think of how division is toxic, Division disfigures the face of the church, division is a church scandal that lacks in unity is ignoring the body of Christ, and it scandalizes Jesus' name, therefore resulting in further insult to God. If you think not having unity is not a sin-then you need to think again. The kingdom is continuation, it's continuous, not to be discontinued for lack of the church body. This division makes for a ministry mess, ministry madness, a ministry menace to the kingdom, division is dysfunctional, and unbiased to the Christ. Acting in a manner that's relegated and designated to mess. As they say on the streets, "you throwing shade acting shady"! Well **Psalm 91** says *He that dwelleth in the secret place of the most High shall abide under the shadow of the Almighty.* So, this is the covenant we should ALL remember to be operating and carrying out, for adequate ministry functionally.

As well it goes further on to tell us:

2 I will say of the LORD, He is my refuge and my fortress: my God; in him will I trust.

3 Surely he shall deliver thee from the snare of the fowler, and from the noisome pestilence.

4 He shall cover thee with his feathers, and under his wings shalt thou trust: his truth shall be thy shield and buckler.

5 Thou shalt not be afraid for the terror by night; nor for the arrow that flieth by day;

6 Nor for the pestilence that walketh in darkness; nor for the destruction that wasteth at noonday.

7 A thousand shall fall at thy side, and ten thousand at thy right hand; but it shall not come nigh thee.

I pray we cease this no-good deed of church failures, beginning with those that are supposed to be the body of Christ! Christians? Servants? Saints? Saved? Leaders? Officers? Believers? And every Minister with a title *(of any kind)*?

God has always been interested in our failures, way back on Calvary. Jesus went to the cross as our *corrector*, So God's people are not to be treating the Holy Spirit as something biodegradable BUT rather exalted.

But he was wounded for our transgressions, he was bruised for our iniquities: the chastisement of our peace was upon him; and with his stripes we are healed. **Isaiah 53:5**

Either ALL in - or ALL out! Without hesitating or procrastinating, it's time to act NOW! We've been through many seasons of stumbling blocks, setbacks and obstacles and it's time to move Satan and all his minions out the way and excel the name of Jesus! With humility and dignity, illuminate Him explore His grace and mercy, expand, grow and manifest His greatness. Have more fasting and praying, and holy convocations. Testimonies! Teach His Word-it saves lives; promote His will-it will keep you; introduce how good He is-it will heal you; offer Him-and it will help you! Teach what it is to pray-you will find He answers. God is a sustainer, He redeems, His esteem power speaks life, and we can live through the Holy Spirit alone.

I have three guarantees in life for you: *That you are born – you die – and there is a God!*

The church goes beyond the building we gather to worship in, but within the church it's the Christians the saints meeting ground to bring people into; to experience God; have change and be different; receive breakthroughs, to feel delivered and to be saved. Where Christ is preached, introduced, God is spoken and taught, and the Holy Spirit is present. *We gather to give God praise, glory, honor, to adore Him and give Him thanks and to pray, but in everything by prayer and supplication, with thanksgiving, let your requests be made known to God;* and know the power of prayer in our lives, to talk to God, celebrate, embrace, communicate and interact, feel the Holy Spirit, and receive His power. *But you will receive power when the Holy Spirit has come upon you.* That's our place to fellowship, we take our discipleship outside the walls to people everywhere and anywhere. The God I know and serve is needed everywhere and required everywhere. In the streets, in the home, on the job, in the hospital, in the shelters, in the subways, on the corner, in the supermarket, in our neighborhoods, within the communities, in the suburbs, in the projects, in the precincts, in the banks, in the malls, in our businesses, in our families, children, spouses, and still in the churches.

Let's ALL be one big recruitment ministry, camp out together in holiness and righteousness and share that one common denominator and depositor amongst us ALL – ABBA Father the one who has adopted us ALL as His own. It has to hurt to see people hurt, jobless, homeless, our kids joining gangs before they join the church, how to keep our jails from overflowing rather than having people coming to Christ and living in the overflow. *God's people are the generational curse breakers, the devil back breakers, Satan's neck cracker, the enemy rejecters, giant slayers and demon destroyers-we are not holding a place in hell for anybody.* We are moving mountains we are on the upside of heaven.

Not living with ministry cancer of the Christian body! And not having an infectious disease; toxic or sepsis spirit that's contagious and affecting and contaminating other Christians. You have caught the put the people out the pasture plague and you spreading it to other ministries.

2 Chronicles 7:14 If my people, which are called by my name, shall humble themselves, and pray, and seek my face, and turn from their wicked ways; then will I hear from heaven, and will forgive their sin, and will heal their land. This scripture is Gods warning and reassurance. Key is: IF MY PEOPLE so there is no substitute or buts. - He assures us of what He will fulfill, what He would do. God is faithful to fulfill.

We better start looking at our Christian resume! God has it from start to finish He doesn't don't need to call nobody for references or recommendations to ask or inquire about you! *Your livelihood shows and tells Him ALL.*

The Devil running rampage and we must pray that people's spirits are ignited and that as they say **'stay lit.'** We don't need them to burn out, be blown out, go out, or be put out. *But always burning, blazing, fueling and filled with Holy Ghost fire!*

The church doesn't need Christian cults and people with crooked Christianity. We need discipline which is next to Godliness-we need obedience which is according to God. *As the body needs physical healing the spirit requires a spiritual healing to function and operate in the will of God.*

1 John 4:1 Dear friends, do not believe every spirit, but test the spirits to see whether they are from God, because many false prophets have gone out into the world.

Church is not the place for your "isms" and "schisms" and scams and scandalous ways. Remove malice remove malicious behavior. Hood rats in the church pretending to be holy. It's a place of decency and order, subject and governed by the Holy Spirit. You even have some folks that want to send subliminal messages when they have no substance to their own ungodly and fake actions-ironically want to quote scriptures as their phony evidence.

James 3:17 But the wisdom that is from above is first pure, then peaceable, gentle, and easy to be intreated, full of mercy and good fruits, without partiality, and without hypocrisy.

And the hypocrites, really, they are nothing more than spiritual intruders and invaders I mean *spiritual body snatchers.* Causing a ministry conspiracy, with their conniving and conspiring ways. Bringing ministry complications because they are filled with foolery and nonsense. It's ministry discrimination because of their jezebel, envious, insecure, lust and jealous spirit. Well jealousy and envy all of it is a disease, AND I pray you're healing from it-that you get better-you be well-and it leaves your fleshy body.

Conformity and control need to stop being the force of power within the church. How does arrogant, cocky, passive aggressive, obnoxious and rude be the way we do church! Why are there comical Christians in the church; why are there cynical Christians in the church. Their philosophy of just who God is and His love is twisted. Their spiritual abuse consists of spitting in or slapping Gods people in the face without doing it physically.

1 Timothy 3:2-3 Therefore an overseer must be above reproach, the husband of one wife, sober-minded, self-controlled, respectable, hospitable, able to teach, 3 not a drunkard, not violent but gentle, not quarrelsome, not a lover of money.

Titus 1:7-8 For an overseer, as God's steward, must be above reproach. He must not be arrogant or quick-tempered or a drunkard or violent or greedy for gain, 8 but hospitable, a lover of good, self-controlled, upright, holy, and disciplined.
The body needs to know that the Holy Spirit is not reluctant! So, you can't alter Gods purpose or his plan. Remember God does 'warn' us. We need to level up and stop acting up! God is the teacher and He is looking for a class of Christians. *God is the church corrector, He is a director of perfection and although it is humanly*

impossible that we are or will ever be perfect-we strive to be examples of His perfect will through His ordinances, His mandate and His commands. To continually feast from His tabernacle, make every day feel like Pentecost, to have an upper room experience repeatedly and to make every person feel like resurrection Sunday all over. His resurrection pierces our hearts, and illuminates our minds that when we raise the blood-stained banner we can flip on the Devil, steal his evil thoughts and take back all he stole and show him who's boss and who's large and in charge. Destroy his entire terrible territory. Everybody gets their joy back, their peace back and live victorious-and no longer Satan's victim.

Job 36:11 If they obey and serve him, they will spend the rest of their days in prosperity and their years in contentment.

James 4:7-8 Submit yourselves, then, to God. Resist the devil, and he will flee from you. 8 Come near to God and he will come near to you. Wash your hands, you sinners, and purify your hearts, you double-minded.

Yes! Let's ALL submit and surrender. Have resilience and live in Christ's residence. That's a good place to live, a great place actually. If you need to, relocate to a kingdom place – there's room for everybody, don't worry about the crowd, we need the multitude, the more the merrier. In the process we resist the Devil. Refuse him from residing in your neighborhood or address, we don't want him in our house, on our block on our street! We have a smear campaign against the Devil. We on a Christ crusade-he cannot take part-we have kicked him out from getting ownership where we reside. I'm sorry he was never welcomed in the first place. Didn't he fall from grace! Those who want to take up residency with him-need to vacate, we will issue evictions by the blood of Jesus that flesh is not tolerated or accepted. Therefore, status remains denied!!! We are filling the Kingdom with the saints and the people with qualified applications that are coming to be healed, delivered, and saved, let the redeemed of the Lord say so, that they are looking for new hope, new joy and new peace. That is found at the cross. The grateful gathering. *There's a naked world out here, and we need to clothe and dress them with the Love and Word of God!* We come to church to experience God – But we go out into the world to promote the Word of God.

Putting God first and keeping God first as told in **Matthew 6:33** *But seek ye first the kingdom of God, and his righteousness; and all these things shall be added unto you.*

Let the people come-one and ALL every age. Let's begin to repair the world person by person. Spreading the gospel, I am not ashamed of the gospel of Jesus Christ. Take the church to the people bring them into the church and send them out-proclaiming and sharing and winning. If we want a change; a God life change for the world, if we want transformation and to reach every population, a paradigm shift; then form ministries that will supply and give back.

The churches have to connect with the local precincts and the communities they serve. Spread and rebrand to reach out to a lost, hurt, sick, broken, unchartered and dying world. We have victims, people struggling with sickness, ailments and diseases, we have addicts, we have drugs, and gang issues and violence, people losing homes, and fires, thieves, murderers, rapist, pedophiles, molesters, incest, racism, racial profiling, suicide, divorce.

We have domestic violence, disabilities, we have all kinds of abuse, sex trafficking, kidnapping, people grieving, mourning, family matters, job issues, infertility, corruption, pollution, disasters, crisis etc. and a country in trouble, nations with troubles and just a world of problems all around no matter where we are where we go. *World War Us! BUT we have a God whose omnipresence and omnipotence overshadow the enemy, so we have it ALL and that's ALL the world needs to be introduced to and to know Him. He will change the trajectory* – we need to be that conduit between Him and them. Call me what you want – BUT I refuse to disbelieve or feel that it is that impossible to reach and teach people through the love of Christ to save and redeem them. I believe in the miracle working God. That with the right approach; the right appearance; the right time; the right place; the right people; the right words and the love of God that is so irresistible, that we can try without ceasing without hesitation, BUT it will take togetherness, to win more souls for Christ! Even for the fornicators and the backsliders. This world depends on it! God is depending on us!

Matthew 28:19 Go therefore and make disciples of all the nations [help the people to learn of Me, believe in Me, and obey My words], baptizing them in the name of the Father and of the Son and of the Holy Spirit,

GIVING TITHE & OFFERINGS

W e must know that as well as giving of ourselves we need to give in our giving. We must tithe as Christians, if you say you trust and believe God; then give your tithes cheerfully as the Lord requires and let Him work out the other 90% for you to pay your bills, eat and provide for your families. Tithing is part of being saved [tithe translates to a tenth]. God's Word has plenty to say about giving.

His generosity alone should compel us to give willingly and generously. God offered His Son-and we should offer a monetary sacrifice to help our churches strive and bless the kingdom. Our tithes will enable our churches to build and grow that when in times needed, they are prepared to give back and help. Our Churches should and could be the biggest banks. Aren't we above and not beneath; the lenders and not the borrowers; the head and not the tail; as well we are the givers and not the takers? We put thousands, millions into designer clothing and foot wear-why aren't we putting and investing into the kingdom. Not just tithing we should be increasing our offerings. The best offer I have is to the one who paid it ALL. Since we can never re-pay him; we certainly can continuously thank Him through our tithes and offerings. Let's ALL be a part of spiritual giving.

Genesis 14:19-20

19 And he blessed him, and said, Blessed be Abram of the most high God, possessor of heaven and earth:

20 And blessed be the most high God, which hath delivered thine enemies into thy hand. And he gave him tithes of all.

Numbers 18:21

21 And, behold, I have given the children of Levi all the tenth in Israel for an inheritance, for their service which they serve, even the service of the tabernacle of the congregation.

Deuteronomy 14:22

22 Thou shalt truly tithe all the increase of thy seed, that the field bringeth forth year by year.

2 Chronicles 31:4-5

4 Moreover he commanded the people that dwelt in Jerusalem to give the portion of the priests and the Levites, that they might be encouraged in the law of the LORD.

5 And as soon as the commandment came abroad, the children of Israel brought in abundance the firstfruits of corn, wine, and oil, and honey, and of all the increase of the field; and the tithe of all things brought they in abundantly.

Malachi 3:8-10

8 Will a man rob God? Yet ye have robbed me. But ye say, Wherein have we robbed thee? In tithes and offerings.

9 Ye are cursed with a curse: for ye have robbed me, even this whole nation.

10 Bring ye all the tithes into the storehouse, that there may be meat in mine house, and prove me now herewith, saith the LORD of hosts, if I will not open you the windows of heaven, and pour you out a blessing, that there shall not be room enough to receive it.

Only the Devil tries to rob God! And evaporate and zap us from God's work. The Lord loves a cheerful giver! We are His off spring, His creation, a mirror image and carbon copy and we need to give diligently and willingly to our churches and to bless our Shepherds, leaders and overseers who continuously pour out into us and feed us the Word of God. Delivering, teaching and admonishing us through every sermon every message that His Word is true.

Jeremiah 3:15
And I will give you pastors/shepherds according to/after mine heart, which shall feed you with knowledge and understanding.

LIVING PAST/BEYOND THE HURT

And this is what I will do! "Bless the Lord AT ALL TIMES!" This means no matter what I am going through, no matter what situation I am in, no matter what I face, no matter the circumstance, no matter the place I am in or the place that I am at! YES! Even in the hurt I was experiencing in the church-*I WILL* become ALL I can say… I can't say for nobody else, but I can say for me "THAT I WILL BLESS THE LORD AT ALL TIMES!" Even in the difficult times, the painful times I thought would never go away and I still said I WILL!!! *That it wasn't said as my testimony it was my only philosophy to BLESS THE LORD AT ALL TIMES!*

Psalm 34
I will bless the LORD at all times: his praise shall continually be in my mouth.

2 My soul shall make her boast in the LORD: the humble shall hear thereof, and be glad.

3 O magnify the LORD with me, and let us exalt his name together.

4 I sought the LORD, and he heard me, and delivered me from all my fears.

5 They looked unto him and were lightened: and their faces were not ashamed.

6 This poor man cried, and the LORD heard him, and saved him out of all his troubles.

When there was nothing I could do; even when there was nothing more for me to say; nothing left for me to say; nothing I can think to say-it was only I WILL BLESS THE LORD AT ALL TIMES. When I was feeling sorrow, down, castrated in spirit, a spiritual attack, broken spirits, dissolved spirits, assassinated spirits, dead spirits, mutilated spirits, executed spirits, persecuted spirits, that my spirits were ambushed and I was bamboozled right from the place that delayed, rejected and denied me. The place that HURT ME!

I did what the Holy Spirit auctioned in me. I know I am being judged that I was serving man and not God because I left-But those who know me also know that is the furthest from the truth. That my twelve years there and my seven-year hiccup that through it ALL – I honored, adored and loved the Lord most! I just still respected authority, I tried, I stayed in place, I was obedient, I improvised, and I sacrificed., I served and I remained empathetic as a parishioner, a Christian and a member.

Psalm 27:14 Wait on the LORD: be of good courage, and he shall strengthen thine heart: wait, I say, on the LORD.
My dignity kept me as president of the ministry I served, my ability kept me on as one of the intercessors. Because Great is THY Faithfulness. Being a servant is always

trusting and believing God in all things. It's almost like taking vows or an oath. It's a lifetime commitment. You have to work hard, stay prepared as best you can, and always keep God first in whatever you deal with as well everything you do. Not to compromise but to strategize. So, if the service you are in, that you attend has been compromised - do know that the Holy Spirit is no longer present! With the absence of the Holy Spirit there is no fellowship. *Without our praise there is no presence and without His presence there is no worship!* We are worshippers and we give praises in the name of God-for the Lord inhabits the praises of HIS people. We praise, shout, rejoice, give glory, we sing praises we reverence in His presence, we invite His presence, we give thanks. We don't ignore and then rid the Holy Spirit – there's no acceptance to fake worshipping.

2 Peter 2:21 For it had been better for them not to have known the way of righteousness, than, after they have known it, to turn from the holy commandment delivered unto them.

See, I could not bring myself to turn from the merciful and righteous God! I will never understand how people can become saved, believe God, read His Word and still do things unholy. I can't get with the contradictory mind set. God is not temporary or is He ordinary-but He is forever and extraordinary. The 'so called Christians must remain and those that never knew Him, are the ones we are supposed to be going after. How you a Christian on Sunday and the Devil on Monday; and live the rest of the week like hell and treated your fellow Christians on Sunday as less than! *See I'm just saying.*

In **Mark** He tells us that *Satan comes immediately* in *4:15.* That means He's coming with power to! A satanic attack, a demonic force. We may think he's a joke and take him as a joke-but he's real. And everything you know and everything you do as a believer he does; he was praising before us. Know he's good at it! Our position is to be better at it. So those that want to muscle you, mute you, and strong hold you-be aware. The Devil uses them to accomplish and succeed in violating you, making you feel dispensable, treating you like the Devil's personal S&M and I do not mean saved and manifestation. Judas spirits all around, yuck spirits all around.

2 Corinthians 10:5 We destroy arguments and every lofty opinion raised against the knowledge of God, and take every thought captive to obey Christ,

Like I said I was in the fight of my life. And once you start retrieving the word of God even in **Hebrews 10:32** *But call to remembrance the former days, in which, after ye were illuminated, ye endured a great fight of afflictions;* It was spiritual strangulation, the Devil was trying to choke Christ right out my life. But I was about to fight back with all the calamity coming at me. I was ridiculed and subject to the demolishment devil. BUT I can't and I won't let this temporary ministry madness interrupt and affect my permanent blessings...... The enemy tried to remove me, destroy me, affect my anointing, my word, my joy, my peace, my victory, my salvation, kill my love, take away my marriage, tried to take the church out of me-NO Devil you can't separate me and my husband and you can't take the church out of me. *I'm going to remain radical for Christ, there's liberty in my praise there's freedom in my worship.* [The Devil had to learn who he was messing with] I advise you to develop a life in Christ, watch prosperity manifest.

Psalm 139:23-24 Search me, O God, and know my heart: try me, and know my thoughts: 24 And see if there be any wicked way in me, and lead me in the way everlasting.

HURT is a dangerous thing! It's about one of the worst things to happen to anybody being hurt! That if you don't get help it will cause your mind to erupt; your heart to destruct; your soul to corrupt and your life to suffer. *I report to work five days a week. I work with the best group of doctors practicing medicine on this side of heaven – I just love how they are noble, self-sacrificing, ethical, their kind, caring, concern, compassion toward every patient comes first! How is it, the Christians come to church and not put God first? We need to stop the hurting and have more healing and helping as God's people.

I struggled and had concerns with going to another church and thought maybe just show up on Sunday service and then leave – because I was left feeling and wondering that those in attendance would not care if I was there or not. Why would anyone else want me? But I heard the Lord say ignore those problems - which become my promises and I am not a man that I should lie. I am your God LO I AM WITH YOU - it was 'speak Lord speak!'

Well everyone I guess fears the Lord differently, so this is why I removed my Spirit to save my soul. Deflective and defective, deviating from the divinity, defrauding the divinity of an awesome God. We need to stop with the reckless behavior in the church. Believe the day of reckoning will be coming before we totally wreck the details of scripture in the Old Testament. Recklessness will never bring revelation.

1 Corinthians 1:18 Christ Crucified Is God's Power and Wisdom For the message/preaching of the cross is foolishness to those who are perishing, but to us who are being saved it is the power of God.

On top of my spiritual ill treatment. I was diagnosed in 2009 with an intestinal illness called Gastroparesis, as well I had gallstones and had Cholecystectomy surgery that March. I was also diagnosed with IBS [Irritable Bowel Syndrome} and I have been living with this condition since. BUT GOD! Now I share that because one of the triggers outside of food is stress-So I agitated my condition do to the fact I was dealing with spiritual stress within. That I gave my IBS a new name [I won't mention]. Not a nice thing to say but it's what I felt. Then I just had to let it go and let God!!! Leave the brokenness behind and move on to be put back together, repaired, restored, revived, and reconnected.

We all should feel like honorariums when we come in the sanctuary.

I really want to say: let's not badger and mistreat people within the walls of any church. We need the prophetic not the pathetic. No more than we should mistreat people period. It's just further detrimental to go through this in a church. You have to pick yourself up, dust off the hurt particles and keep it moving. I was punishing myself instead of purifying by staying and pleasing the enemy. The venom and the poison have to stay off of God's people. I wasn't soaking and bathing there anymore; I wasn't basking in His presence. I thank God for strength, courage, grace and mercy keeping me along the way while I was there. **What are we declaring and decreeing if we are busy degrading and disgracing?**

Acts 14:23 And when they had appointed elders for them in every church, with prayer and fasting they committed them to the Lord in whom they had believed.

None of us are Christian geniuses, but when you are born again you strive for greatness and you seek improvement. From the life orchestrator and illustrator that's why He's author and finisher, beginning and the end, He's Alpha and Omega. Let's redefine how we do church. Think of how Paul persecuted the church against God But that Damascus experience changed him forever. That is an experience that I hope we all encounter or will soon encounter. The name changes Saul to Paul was the conversion. Why? Because of change. How he gets baptized, he preaches Christ is the Son of God; he escapes death and he goes into Jerusalem and how he caused the church to prosper.

Acts 9:31 Then the churches throughout all Judea, Galilee, and Samaria had peace and were edified. And walking in the fear of the Lord and in the comfort of the Holy Spirit, they were multiplied.

I relate to Paul as my changed experience is something I'll never forget and it's certainly something I treasure that I look to see that others become of the same. So, I was able to move past my setback amongst the Hellenist just as Paul in spite of; we need a holy convocation, we need true devotion, we need people to be saturated in the blood and consecrated with His love. To accelerate, motivate and elevate God's kingdom – we need to feel the power to just believe and achieve.

I love how Christian songs, devotional songs, secular songs that the gospel artists put out and the church choirs. How spiritual music does something for you how it resonates and gets down deep in you and you play and rehearse the songs in your head repeatedly. You shout alone and cry out to God through some of them, singing at the top of your voice even if you off key but the song is everything. Christian music gives life it enhances our soul. It makes you come alive it feeds your mind, I just love all the gospel artists and gospel greats-I love my Christian music! But I have to admit: I love Lil Duval when he says *I'm living my best life; I'm not going back and forth with you ---- --.* Well I say **'I'm living my Christ life; I'm not going back and forth with you Devils.'**

I was physically, emotionally and spiritually in the fight of my life, fighting to go to church and fighting to stay in the church and even when I was gone it was still a fight in me because my husband was still there and I was fighting within myself wanting him to leave too when God had already spoken. Remember I said earlier [conviction-mine, not his].

Philippians 3:13-14 Brethren, I count not myself to have apprehended: but this one thing I do, forgetting those things which are behind, and reaching forth unto those things which are before, 14 I press toward the mark for the prize of the high calling of God in Christ Jesus.

In living past the hurt: I had to have a new revelation that God revealed to me that going after someone that bad for a piece of paper was a spiritual travesty. God took away the hurt to say I have qualified you! I'm well pleased with your credentials; I know your love for me and for my people; I will send you to a church. To place you back in the worship and fellowship you desire. Don't worry about being licensed you won't have to be afraid of nobody, you won't have to beg nobody, second guess nobody, you won't need to sleep with nobody, creep with nobody, lay with nobody, deceive nobody, or even step on nobody, mislead nobody, mistreat nobody, hate on nobody or hurt anybody.

CHURCH HOME FOR ME *John 17:8 For I have given them the words that you gave me, and they have received them and have come to know in truth that I came from you; and they have believed that you sent me.*

I know being a leader is never easy or is it convenient! How hard Bishops and Pastors, etc. all have it! I fully get the tasks and I myself can never do it! I am designed and cut out to be under someone's authority since I have always wanted that. I know how they are put under a microscope and subject to so much scrutiny, but I believe in praying for them, up lifting them and the capacity they fill.

Hebrews 13:17 Obey your leaders and submit to them, for they are keeping watch over your souls, as those who will have to give an account. Let them do this with joy and not with groaning, for that would be of no advantage to you.

Encouraging and supporting one another is a valuable part of our Christian walk. How much more important is it then to affirm and bless our pastors and spiritual leaders with words, scriptures and acts of appreciation, kindness, love, generosity and gratification?

1 Peter 5:2-3 shepherd the flock of God that is among you, exercising oversight, not under compulsion, but willingly, as God would have you; not for shameful gain, but eagerly; 3 not domineering over those in your charge, but being examples to the flock.

Acts 14:23 And when they had appointed elders for them in every church, with prayer and fasting they committed them to the Lord in whom they had believed.

I pray my church home becomes my pillar and banner real soon to prevent further hurt. It hurts not to be under someone's tutelage and to have transparency as a student of the gospel forever. So, I need to be in great worship and fellowship. I am a worshipper. I give praise by nature and I serve the Lord. I am a new creature in Christ, I embrace the Holy Spirit, I welcome in the Holy Spirit [don't you know that it's readily available waiting on us – to become one with us]. The aroma of GOD! *(The enemy stinks so bad he makes me sick when he comes around. I have an allergic reaction to his stench as my spirit reacts.* I want the smell of goodness-I smell HIS presence in the atmosphere. There is such a sweet anointing about the oil of God, that God is intentional, He's affectionate and full of emotions so I believe coming out of darkness into His marvelous light. He's shelters me from the storm, and He's a way maker, a promise keeper and a burden bearer. The prince of peace overshadows the prince of darkness and every principality. We are more than conquers; we are able to overcome any thing through our Lord who is our strength. And when you read:

Psalm 27

The LORD is my light and my salvation; whom shall I fear? the LORD is the strength of my life; of whom shall I be afraid?

2 When the wicked, even mine enemies and my foes, came upon me to eat up my flesh, they stumbled and fell.

3 Though an host should encamp against me, my heart shall not fear: though war should rise against me, in this will I be confident.

4 One thing have I desired of the LORD, that will I seek after; that I may dwell in the house of the LORD all the days of my life, to behold the beauty of the LORD, and to enquire in his temple.

5 For in the time of trouble he shall hide me in his pavilion: in the secret of his tabernacle shall he hide me; he shall set me up upon a rock.

6 And now shall mine head be lifted up above mine enemies round about me: therefore will I offer in his tabernacle sacrifices of joy; I will sing, yea, I will sing praises unto the LORD.

7 Hear, O LORD, when I cry with my voice: have mercy also upon me, and answer me.

8 When thou saidst, Seek ye my face; my heart said unto thee, Thy face, LORD, will I seek.

9 Hide not thy face far from me; put not thy servant away in anger: thou hast been my help; leave me not, neither forsake me, O God of my salvation.

10 When my father and my mother forsake me, then the LORD will take me up.

11 Teach me thy way, O LORD, and lead me in a plain path, because of mine enemies.

12 Deliver me not over unto the will of mine enemies: for false witnesses are risen up against me, and such as breathe out cruelty.

13 I had fainted, unless I had believed to see the goodness of the LORD in the land of the living.

14 Wait on the LORD: be of good courage, and he shall strengthen thine heart: wait, I say, on the LORD.

As well we are told in **Philippians 4:13** *I can do all things through Christ which strengtheneth me.* Just as I lived beyond the hurt-You can live past your hurt…. *Know that to hurt is temporary, hurting is just preparing and that you will heal and recover real soon.* Our only help is in the Master, the King, in God himself and nobody else. Just as we know the enemy shows up immediately! God shows up immediately! He protects, He covers, He shields so who do you trust? My leaving had to take place, because in life we learn lessons as well as life is lessons learned. Yes, I grew up in this church! BUT was I growing in this church? OR, did this church outgrow me? The answer I received was, it just was not the church for me! I would replay daily the song *'Your Will'* by Darius Brooks. One of the best spiritual healing songs ever…

God tests our spirits, but He never teases our spirits. Only the devil tempts-I'm not falling into filthy temptation. Surviving the hurt, living beyond the hurt – I knew God, I know Him and I know I still will make Him known to others. *That His WORD is Life-My Life is His Word*. I believe in the blood of Jesus; I believe He died for us and He rose again on the third day, I believe in baptism of water, I believe Jesus is the Son of God, I believe in the Father Son and Holy Spirit, I believe now and forever that He saves. So, I will say this: *Bless the LORD, O my soul: and all that is within me, bless his holy name. **Psalm 103:1***

God Be With You….

CLOSING

I must say this lastly as a tribute to moving through, past and beyond the hurt. That I can hear my Mama singing one of her favorite hymns: "My Hope is built on nothing less than Jesus blood and righteousness-I dare not trust the sweetest frame, but wholly lean on Jesus name. On Christ the solid rock I stand all other ground is sinking sand…"

I want to share my 'MAMA' moment with you. I call it: **'Mama Story'** *Allean Ruth McCain Merriwether*

GOD HAS CALLED ME TO BE DIFFERENT….
During the most difficult time in my life!!!!!

Let me share when my calling became clear. On November 9th 2015 MAMA went in the hospital with a blood infection from her dialysis port. Oh, I never knew that the most difficult time in my life, God would be calling me to be different. After a month of all she went through, on December 6th that I and my four-year-old granddaughter went to the hospital and the Lord was CLEAR! He allowed me to say something I thought I'd never say. That if she lives another moment, another minute, another day, another week, another month, another year-I'm just going to be thankful. I couldn't say this when my grandfather got ill, I couldn't say it when my uncle was suffering from HIV, I couldn't say it when cancer afflicted my aunt, I couldn't say it when my brother's death was ruled a suicide. BUT, after MAMA laid there in that hospital at 92 years of age, constantly on antibiotics, pacemaker in her heart, kidney failure, low blood pressure.

The Lord began a new process-a new call-HE reminded me how HE blessed her to see five (5) generations [*Glory to HIS name*]. On Christmas morning they called to tell us they were taking her into MICU-now she can't breathe and NO blood pressure reading at all-they intubated her with a breathing tube and feeding tube. I can only say Jesus breathes new life and your blood run through her. Then he reminded me how His strength is made perfect; and Mama is good! And I just witnessed that she spent the last three days talking to every deceased family member and living her past life right before us.

That if I wasn't a believer, and I am that certainly it will make anyone a believer. *Psalms 116:15 Precious in the sight of the LORD is the death of his saints.* That even on December 21st she told us she was the first and the last. I knew what she meant about the last, but I didn't know what she meant about the first [yes, she's the last of her 17 siblings]. Then on December 29th we made the painful decision to put her in Palliative care. My-my- my. Although painful God said I'll sustain you. Then on December 31st I heard the voice of Jesus say go out to watch night my child, Mama will live to see a new year, after the doctors told my mother, uncle and cousin she won't make it through the day. I didn't receive it because I had an assurance. They all decided they would stay the night. I went to service, Pastor prayed, and God was still speaking…. The next morning, I got a text from my cousin

– he said, "cuz I wanna go with you and your husband to the hospital I have to see my last auntie." OHHHH God revealed to me that Mama was leaving this earthly place today confirmation that was her 1st!!!!!! We arrived at the hospital Palliative Unit at 5pm {grace} I just couldn't get it together that day to get up there earlier {*ohh you can imagine what I was going through*}. But God! My husband, my cuz and I walked into Mama's room #5 {grace} my aunt and uncle on each side the bed. I went to rubbing on her head telling her Mama I love you, and all she's done; it's going to be alright.

Me, my husband, my aunt and uncle and cuz. Five of us in the room {triple grace}. I started to hear something I've never heard before-I bent down closer to her chest. I said I heard about people taking their last breath, My God is this it. Jesus said yes, she's transitioning and you are transforming. The world seemed to stop became silent to me. I raised up the machines going. The doctor walked in to assess and examined her and said I'm sorry she has transitioned. I began praying. After all that, Jesus was clear to me that her accession is for me to be different!!!!

You see I was called in the past to change – and I did. I just didn't complete what God requested of me. Now that God has called me to be different, I will complete what is required of me.

I never thought that when I took the Call of God class that God would reveal the ultimate challenge in my life-that mentally, emotionally, physically and spiritually.

MY MAMA would be called home. He called me to be different!!!! I had her 49 years of my life. Master Jesus is on the thrown and He's making his request known.

Loving Christ! Loving Life!!!

CPSIA information can be obtained
at www.ICGtesting.com
Printed in the USA
LVHW010900300920
667476LV00005B/337